LABORATORY Manual

MATHEMATICS

CBSE Class X

LABORATORY Manual

MATHEMATICS

CBSE Class X

Authors
Rakesh Pandey, Hewanti Kushwaha

Name..

Class........................ Section....................... Roll No......................

School..

Arihant Prakashan (School Division Series)

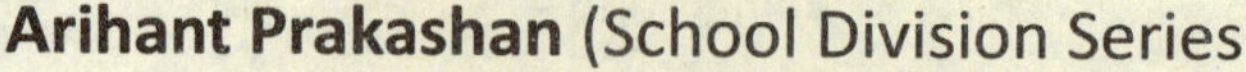

Arihant Prakashan (School Division Series)

Administrative & Production Offices

Regd. Office
'Ramchhaya' 4577/15, Agarwal Road, Darya Ganj, New Delhi -110002
Tele: 011- 47630600, 43518550; Fax: 011- 23280316

Head Office
Kalindi, TP Nagar, Meerut (UP) - 250002, Tele: 0121-7156203, 7156204

Sales & Support Offices
Agra, Ahmedabad, Bengaluru, Bareilly, Chennai, Delhi, Guwahati, Hyderabad, Jaipur, Jhansi, Kolkata, Lucknow, Nagpur & Pune

Price : ₹ 350.00

PO No. : TXT-59-T069476-2-26

Published by Arihant Publications (India) Ltd.

For further information about the books from Arihant, log on to **www.arihantbooks.com** or email to **info@arihantbooks.com**

Follow us on   

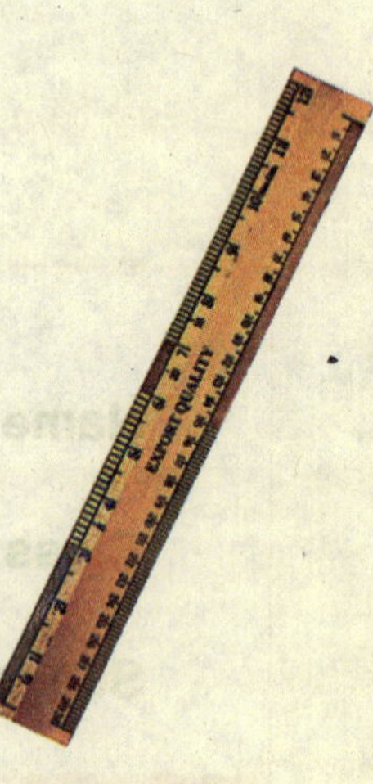

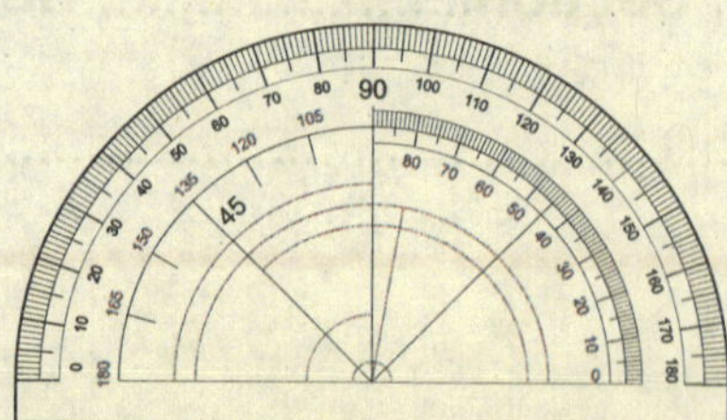

Contents

LIST OF ACTIVITIES

LIST OF PROJECTS

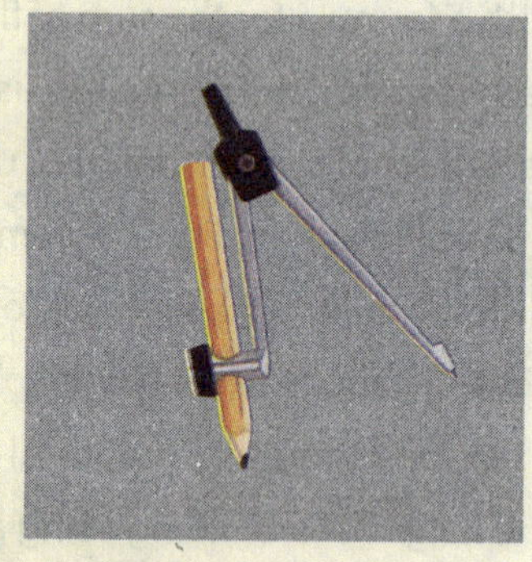

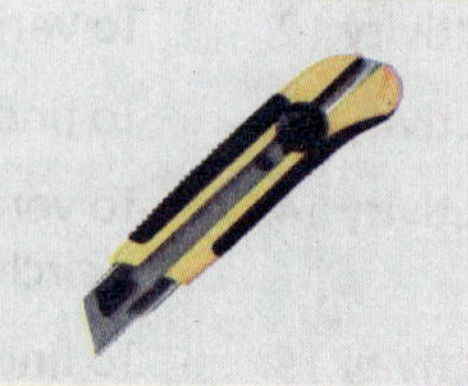
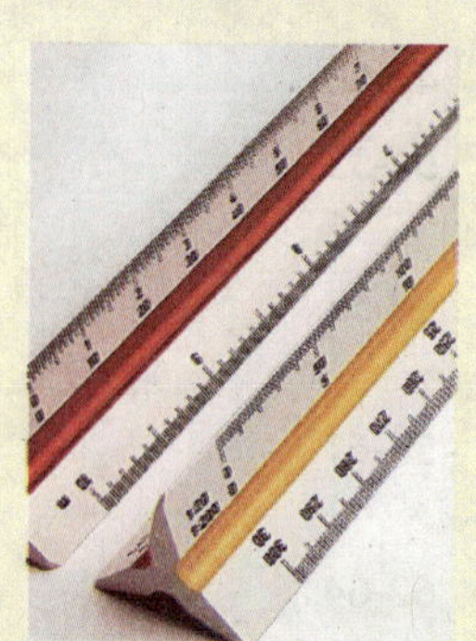
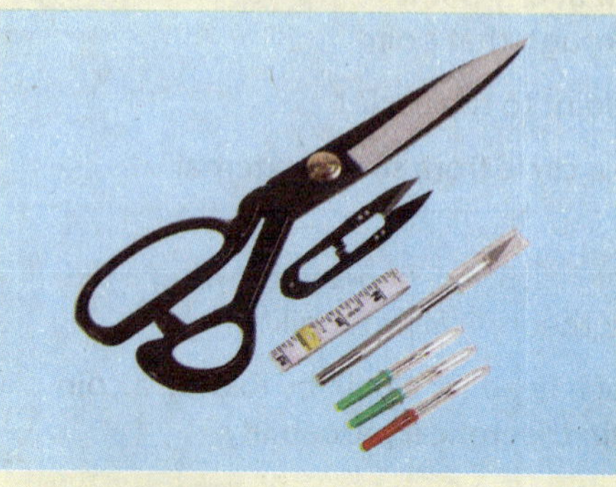
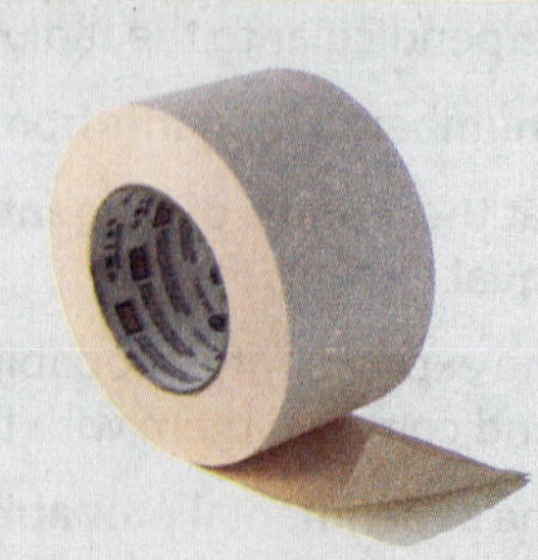

INDEX

S.No.	Name of the Activity/Project	Page No.	Date	Remarks

INDEX

S.No.	Name of the Activity/Project	Page No.	Date	Remarks

LABORATORY Manual

MATHEMATICS

CERTIFICATE

This is to certify that Activities & Projects recorded in this Practical Notebook have been performed by ______________________
(Student's name)

of __________ of ______________________________
(class/section) (school name)

during academic session ______________________

.... Examiner Signature

.... Principal Signature (with school stamp)

.... Teacher Signature

The Purpose of The Mathematics Laboratory

The main objective of mathematics is to train the students to think and analysis the given situations and act logically. These objectives can only be achieved if there is an opportunity of creating a scope of exploring, verifying and experimenting upon mathematical results by students themselves.

Since, activities create interest among students who wants to explore and test some of their ideas, beliefs about mathematics and also present a problem or a challenge with the possibility of generating futher challenges and problems.

Mathematics laboratory is a place where scientific research and experiments are conducted for verification, exploration or discovery. The role of laboratory is helpful in understanding the mathematical concepts, formulae through activities.

A mathematics laboratory can foster mathematical awareness, skill building, positive attitude and learning by doing experiments in various topics of mathematics such as Algebra, Geometry, Mensuration, Coordinate Geometry, etc. It is the place where students can generate problem and struggle to a answer and learn certain concepts using concrete objects and verify many mathematical facts and properties using models, measurements and other activities.

The laboratory will act as a forum for the teachers to discuss and deliberate on some important mathematical issues and problems of the day.

Mathematics laboratory is expected to offer the following opportunities to learners:

- To discover the pattern for getting insight into the formulae.
- To visualise algebraic and analytical results geometrically.
- Offers more scope for individual participation. It encourages students to become independent learners.
- To encourage students in recognising, extending, formulating patterns and enabling them to pose problems in the form of conjectures.
- To exhibit relatedness of mathematics with day to day life problems.
- Builds up inherent interest and confidence in the students towards learning and doing mathematics.
- It helps to supplement the knowledge learned in classroom.

Role of Mathematics Laboratory in Teaching-Learning

The mathematics laboratory can contribute in a big way to the learning of this subject. Some of the ways are:

- Here, the student will get an opportunity to understand the abstract ideas/concepts through concrete objects and situations.
- The concepts of cylinder can be easily understood by making working models using rectangular or square paper.
- Height and distances concepts can only be conceived by trigonometric formulae in the laboratory, where as it is very difficult to understand these concepts on a black board.
- The concept of coordinate geometry, becomes very clear by drawing their graphs using mathematical instruments, which can be done in the laboratory.
- Since, the larger time available individually to the student and opportunity to repeat an activity several times, students can revise and rethink the problem and solutions. It helps to develop metacognitive abilities.
- It widens the experiential base and lays groundwork for later learning of new areas of mathematics and helps to make approprite connection between the known and unknown in mathematics.

Management and Maintenance of Laboratory

A laboratory is equipped with instruments, apparatus, equipments, models apart from facilities like water, electricity, etc. Non-availability of a single material or facility out of these may hinder the performance of any experiment activity in the laboratory. Therefore, the laboratory must be well managed and well maintained.

Personal Management and Maintenance

In personal management and maintenance following points are considered:

1. **Cleanliness** A laboratory should always be neat and clean. When students perform experiment activities during the day, it certainly becomes dirty and things are scattered. So, it is the duty of the lab staff to clean the laboratory.
2. **Checking and arranging materials for the day's work** Lab staff should know that what activities are going to be performed on a particular day. The material required for the day's activities must be arranged one day before.
3. The **facilities like water, electricity, etc.** must be checked and made available at the time of experiments.
4. Identify the **necessary materials** required in the laboratory by labeling them with name tags.
5. **Many safety measures** are required while working in laboratory. A list of such measures may be pasted on a wall of the laboratory.
6. Electrification of the laboratory should be professionally done to allow for safety use.
7. A **first aid kit** may be kept in the laboratory.

Management and Maintenance of Materials

To manage and maintain materials for a laboratory following points must be considered:

1. A list of instruments, apparatus, activities and material may be prepared according to the experiments included in the syllabus of mathematics.
2. Arrange the materials in places (on tables, shelves, board, etc) in a way that they can be easily accessed when needed and returned appropriately after use.
3. The instruments, equipments and apparatus should also be checked regularly by the laboratory staff. If any repair is required it should be done immediately.
4. Arrange the benches and tables to allow for free movement in the laboratory.

Materials and Equipments for Mathematics Laboratory

As the students will be involved in a lot of model making activities under the guidance of the teacher, the smooth running of the mathematics laboratory will depend upon the supply of oddments such as strings and threads, cellotape, white cardboard, hardboard, needles and pins, drawing pins, sandpaper, pliers, screwdrivers, rubber bands of different colours, gummed papers and labels, squared papers, plywood, scissors, saw, paint, soldering, solder wire, steel wire, cotton wool, tin and plastic sheets, glazed papers, overhead projector, slide projector etc.

Besides these, some models, charts, slides, etc. made up of a good durable material should also be there for the teacher to demonstrate some mathematical concepts, facts and properties before the students.

Different tables, ready reckner should also be there (in the laminated form) so that these can be used by the students for different purposes.

In view of the above, following is the list of suggested instruments/models for the laboratory:

Equipment

Mathematical instrument set (Wooden Geometry Box for demonstration containing rulers, set-squares, divider, protractor and compasses), some geometry boxes, metre scales of 100 cm, 50 cm and 30 cm, measuring tape, diagonal scale, clinometer, calculators, computers including related software etc.

Models

For demonstration of

- Number System
- Algebra
- Coordinate geometry
- Geometry
- Trigonometry
- Mensuration
- Statistics
- Probability

Activity 1

OBJECTIVE

To draw the graph of a quadratic polynomial and observe:

(i) The shape of the curve, when the coefficient of x^2 is positive.

(ii) The shape of the curve, when the coefficient of x^2 is negative.

(iii) Its number of zeroes.

Prior Knowledge

1. Concept of quadratic polynomial.
2. Graph of the quadratic polynomial.
3. Concept of zeroes.

Materials Required

1. Cardboard
2. Graph papers
3. Ruler
4. Pencil
5. Adhesive

Theory

A polynomial of the form $ax^2 + bx + c$, $a \neq 0$ is called **quadratic polynomial,** where a, b and c are constant.

A **real number** α is said to be a **zero** of a quadratic polynomial $p(x)$, if $p(\alpha) = 0$. Any quadratic equation can have atmost two zeroes.

For any quadratic polynomial $ax^2 + bx + c$, $a \neq 0$, the graph of the corresponding equation $y = ax^2 + bx + c$ has one of the two shapes either **open upwards like** $\cup$ or **open downwards like** $\cap$ (these curves $\cap$ or $\cup$ are called parabolas) depending on whether $a > 0$ or $a < 0$. The zeroes of a polynomial are precisely the x-coordinate of the points, where the graph of polynomial intersects the X-axis. So, the graph of $y = ax^2 + bx + c$, $a \neq 0$, cut the X-axis atmost at two points because it can have atmost two zeroes.

Procedure

1. Paste a graph paper on a cardboard of a suitable size.
2. Consider a quadratic polynomial $p(x) = ax^2 + bx + c$, $a \neq 0$.
3. Two cases arise, either $a > 0$ or $a < 0$.
4. Obtain the points $(x, p(x))$ for some different values of x in the polynomial $p(x) = ax^2 + bx + c$, $(a \neq 0)$.

x	x_1	x_2	x_3	...	x_n
$p(x)$	$p(x_1)$	$p(x_2)$	$p(x_3)$	...	$p(x_n)$

5. Plot all obtained points on the cartesian plane of the graph paper.

6. Now, join these plotted points by a free hand curve to obtain the graph of either type as shown below in Fig. 1.1, Fig. 1.2 and Fig. 1.3.

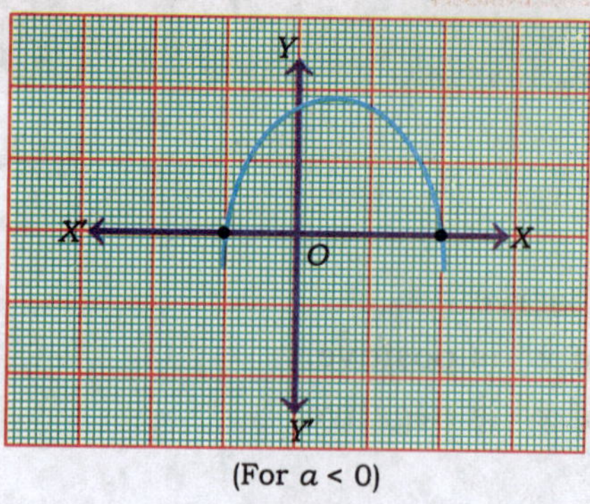

(For $a < 0$)

Fig. 1.1

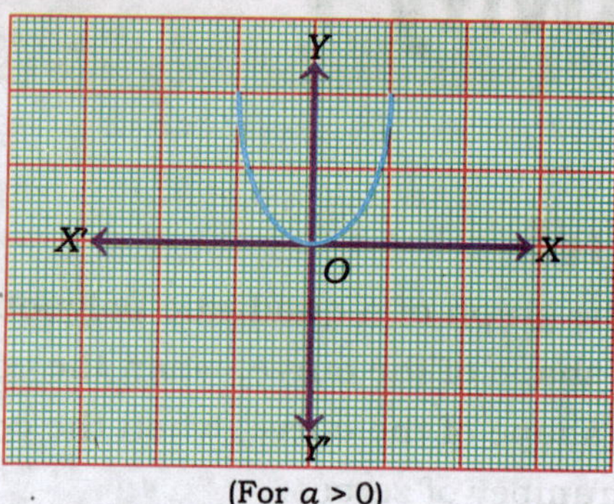

(For $a > 0$)

Fig. 1.2

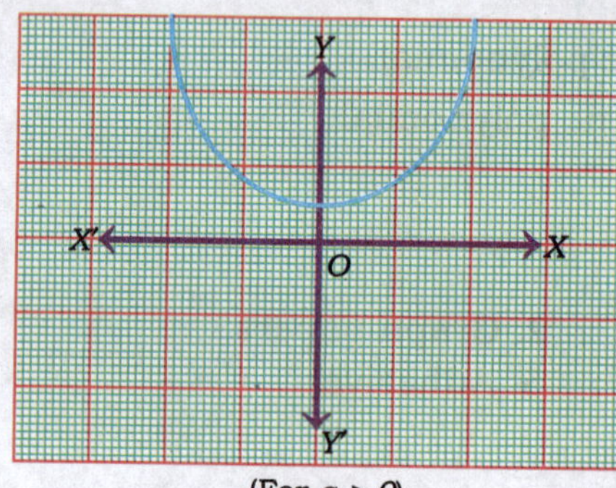

(For $a > 0$)

Fig. 1.3

Demonstration

1. In each case, the shape of the curve is a parabola.
2. When coefficient of x^2 is positive, parabola opens upward. (see Fig. 1.2 and 1.3).
3. When coefficient of x^2 is negative, parabola opens downward. (see Fig. 1.1).
4. Maximum number of zeroes which a quadratic polynomial can have, is 2.
5. Points on the graph paper should be joined by a free hand curve only.

Observations

On actual measurement, we observe that

1. In Fig. 1.1, parabola intersects *X*-axis at ...... point(s).
2. In Fig. 1.1, the number of zeroes of the given polynomial is ....
3. Parabola in Fig. 1.2 intersects *X*-axis at ...... point (s).
4. In Fig. 1.2, the number of zeroes of the given polynomial is ....
5. Parabola in Fig. 1.3 intersects *X*-axis at ...... point (s).
6. In Fig. 1.3, the number of zeroes of the given polynomial is ....

Applications

This activity helps to

1. understand the geometrical representation of a quadratic polynomial.
2. find the number of zeroes of a quadratic polynomial.

Viva-Voce

Q.1 A polynomial of degree 2 can have atmost how many zeroes?

Ans A polynomial of degree 2 can have atmost 2 zeroes.

Q.2 What is the degree of a quadratic polynomial?

Ans The degree of a quadratic polynomial is 2.

Q.3 How many zeroes can a polynomial of degree n have?

Ans A polynomial of degree n can have atmost n zeroes.

Q.4 Number of zeroes of a quadratic polynomial is 1, what will you say about the graph?

Ans Here, the graph will cut the X-axis at exactly one point.

Q.5 What do you understand by geometrical meaning of zeroes of a polynomial?

Ans The zeroes are the x-coordinate of the points, where the graph of polynomial intersects the X-axis.

Q.6 The graph of a quadratic polynomial has a shape of parabola which is open downward. What can you infer from this?

Ans In the equation of quadratic polynomial, the coefficient of x^2 is less than 0.

Q.7 'A graph of a quadratic polynomial intersects the X-axis at 4 points'. Is it true or false?

Ans A quadratic polynomial can have atmost two zeroes, so it can cut X-axis atmost 2 points. So, the given statement is false.

Q.8 What will be the value of m in the polynomial $p(x) = mx^2 - 3(m+1)x - 1$, if 1 is one of its zeroes?

Ans $p(1) = 0 \Rightarrow m(1)^2 - 3(m+1)(1) - 1 = 0 \Rightarrow m - 3m - 3 - 1 \Rightarrow 2m = -4 \Rightarrow m = -2.$

Q.9 What is the relation between its zeroes and coefficients, for a given quadratic polynomial $ax^2 + bx + c$?

Ans If α and β are the zeroes of a quadratic polynomial $ax^2 + bx + c$, then $\alpha + \beta = -\frac{b}{a}$, $\alpha\beta = \frac{c}{a}$.

Q.10 Can $(2x+5)$ be the remainder on division of a polynomial $(8x-65)$? Justify your answer.

Ans No, since degree of $(2x + 5) = 1 =$ degree of $(8x - 65)$.

Activity 2

OBJECTIVE

To identify Arithmetic Progressions in some given lists of numbers (patterns).

Prior Knowledge

Concept of Arithmetic Progression (AP).

Materials Required

1. Cardboard
2. White paper
3. Pen/Pencil
4. Scissors
5. Squared papers
6. Adhesive

Theory

1. An arithmetic progression is a list of numbers, in which each term is obtained by adding a fixed number to the preceding term except the first term.

   This fixed number is called the **common difference** *(d)* of the AP and it can be positive, negative or zero.

   For example, if in the list of numbers $a_1, a_2, a_3, a_4, \ldots$ if the differences $a_2 - a_1$, $a_3 - a_2$, $a_4 - a_3$, ... gives the same value, i.e. if $a_{k+1} - a_k$ is same for different values of k, then the given list of numbers are said to make an **arithmetic progression.**

2. The general form of an AP is $a, a + d, a + 2d, a + 3d, \ldots$

   where, a is the **first term** and d is the **common difference.**

   nth term of an AP is

$$T_n = a + (n - 1)\, d$$

Procedure

1. Take a cardboard of suitable size and paste a white paper on it.
2. Take two squared papers (graph papers) of suitable size and paste them on the cardboard.
3. Let the lists of numbers be

   (i) 1, 2, 5, 9, ... (ii) 2, 5, 8, 11, ...

4. Make strips of lengths 1, 2, 5, 9 units and strips of lengths 2, 5, 8, 11 units and breadth of each strip one unit.

5. Paste the strips of lengths 1, 2, 5, 9 units as shown in Fig. 2.1 and paste the strips of lengths 2, 5, 8,11 units as shown in Fig. 2.2.

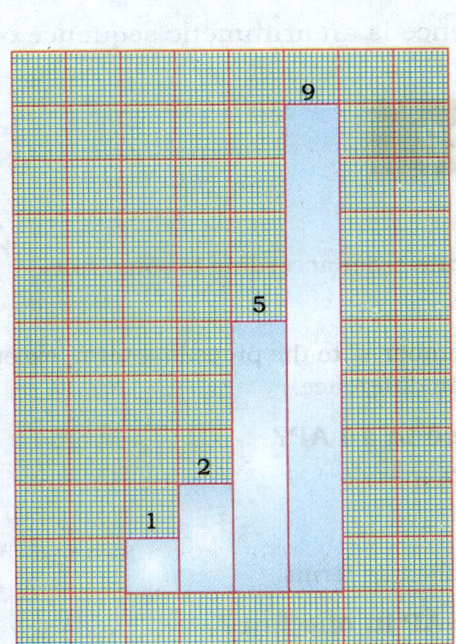

Fig. 2.1

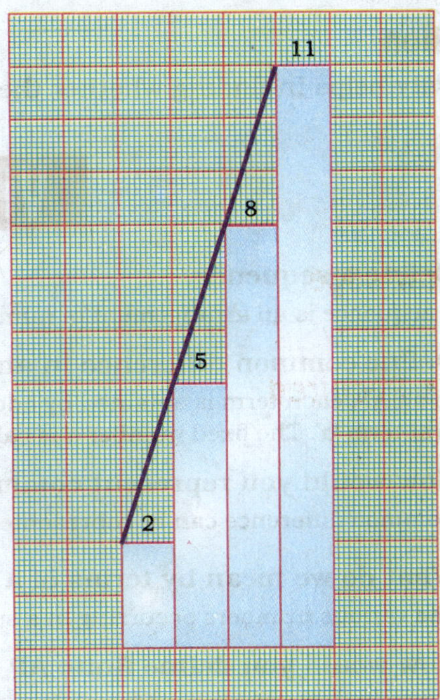

Fig. 2.2

Demonstration

1. In Fig. 2.1, the difference of heights (lengths) of two consecutive strips is not same (uniform). So, it is not an AP.
2. In Fig. 2.2, the difference of heights of two consecutive strips is the same (uniform) throughout. So, it is an AP.
3. In Fig 2.2, we observe that if the left top corners of the strips are joined, they will be in a straight line in case of an AP.

Observation

On actual measurement, we observe that

Figure 2.1	Figure 2.2
The difference of heights of first two strips = ...	The difference of heights of first two strips = ...
The difference of heights of second and third strips = ...	The difference of heights of second and third strips = ...
The difference of heights of third and fourth strips = ...	The difference of heights of third and fourth strips = ...
Difference is not	Difference is ....
So, the list of numbers 1, 2, 5, 9, ... does not form an	So, the list of numbers 2, 5, 8, 11, ... forms an ....

Result

We have identified arithmetic progressions in some given lists of numbers (patterns).

Application

This activity helps in finding whether the given sequence is an arithmetic sequence or not.

Viva-Voce

Q.1 Define a sequence.

Ans A sequence is an arrangement of numbers in a definite order according to some rule.

Q.2 Define common difference in an AP.

Ans In an AP, each term is obtained by adding a fixed number 'd' to the preceding term, except the first term 'a'. The fixed number d is called its common difference.

Q.3 How would you represent common difference in an AP?

Ans Common difference can be represented as $d = a_n - a_{n-1}$.

Q.4 What do we mean by terms of a sequence?

Ans The various numbers occurring in a sequence are called its terms.

Q.5 How would you define finite AP and infinite AP in one line?

Ans If number of terms in an AP is finite, then it is called a finite AP, otherwise it is called an infinite AP.

Q.6 What is the condition for a sequence to be an AP?

Ans There should be equal difference between any two consecutive terms.

Q.7 What is the formula for *n*th term of an AP?

Ans The formula for nth term of an AP is $T_n = a + (n - 1)d$.

Q.8 Let us consider an AP 1, 3, 5, 7, ... If we add 1 in each sequence, will the common difference also increased by 1.

Ans No, the common difference will be remain same.

Q.9 What number should be inserted between *a* and *b* such that three numbers are in AP?

Ans The required number is $\frac{a+b}{2}$.

Q.10 If we multiply each term of an AP with a constant *k*, then what kind of new list of numbers will be obtained?

Ans The new list of numbers will also be form an AP.

Activity 3

OBJECTIVE

To find the sum of first n natural numbers.

Prior Knowledge

1. Concept of natural numbers.
2. Concept of Arithmetic Progression (AP).
3. Concept of the sum of n terms of an AP.

Materials Required

1. Cardboard
2. Coloured papers
3. White papers
4. Cutter
5. Adhesive

Theory

1. Numbers which are used for counting, i.e. 1, 2, 3, 4, ... are called **natural numbers**. Smallest natural numbers is 1 but we cannot find the largest natural number as successor of even natural number is again a natural number. The collection of natural numbers is denoted by N.

   $\therefore \qquad N = \{1, 2, 3, 4, ...\}$
2. For concept of Arithmetic Progression (AP) see Activity 2.
3. For an AP, sum of its n terms is given by

   $$S_n = \frac{n}{2}[2a + (n - 1)d]$$

   where, a = first term of an AP, d = common difference and n = number of terms

   Natural numbers 1, 2, 3, 4, ..., n represents an AP because the difference between two consecutive terms is 1, i.e. constant.

   So, to find the sum of all natural numbers upto n or first n natural numbers, we can apply the formula for the sum of n terms of an AP.

   $$\therefore \qquad S_n = \frac{n}{2}[2a + (n - 1)\ d]$$

   Here, a = first term = 1 and d = common difference = 1

   $$\therefore \qquad S_n = \frac{n}{2}[2 \times 1 + (n - 1)\ 1] = \frac{n}{2}[2 + n - 1] = \frac{n}{2}[n + 1]$$

Procedure

1. Take a rectangular cardboard of suitable size and paste a coloured paper on it.
2. Let us find the sum of first 10 natural numbers (n = 10), i.e. from 1 to 10, so draw a rectangle $ABCD$ of length 10 units (n) and breadth 11 units (n + 1).
3. Divide this rectangle into unit squares (square has side 1 unit) as shown in Fig. 3.1.

4. Starting from upper left-most corner, shade one square, 2 squares, 3 squares and so on. (see Fig. 3.1).

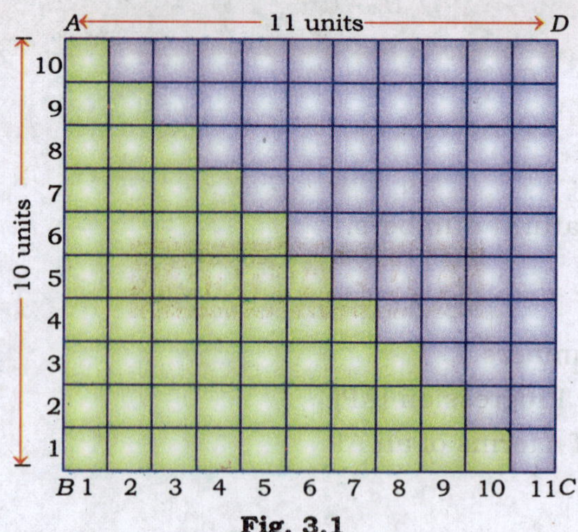

Fig. 3.1

Demonstration

1. The shaded colour region looks like a stair case.
2. Length of 1st stair is 1 unit, length of 2nd stair is 2 units, length of 3rd stair is 3 units, and so on, length of 10th stair is 10 units.
3. These lengths give a pattern 1, 2, 3, 4, ..., 10, which is an AP with first term 1 and common difference 1.
4. Sum of first 10 terms = 1 + 2 + 3 + ... + 10 = 55 ...(i)
5. We observe that

$$\text{Area of the shaded region} = \frac{1}{2} \times \text{Area of rectangle } ABCD = \frac{1}{2} \times \text{Length} \times \text{Breadth}$$

$$= \frac{1}{2} \times 10 \times 11 = 55$$

which is same as obtained in Eq. (i) above.

This shows that the sum of the first 10 natural numbers is $\frac{1}{2} \times 10 \times 11 = \frac{1}{2} \times 10(10+1)$.

This result can be generalised to find the sum of first n natural numbers, as

$$S_n = \frac{1}{2} n(n+1) \quad \text{...(ii)}$$

Observations

On actual measurement, we observe that

On putting $n = 4$ in Eq. (ii), we get S_n = ...

On putting $n = 12$ in Eq. (ii), we get S_n = ...

On putting $n = 50$ in Eq. (ii), we get S_n = ...

On putting $n = 100$ in Eq. (ii), we get S_n = ...

Result

We have found the sum of first n natural numbers.

Applications

1. This result can be used to find the sum of first n natural numbers.
2. This result is useful in researches related to larger natural numbers.

Viva-Voce

Q.1 **Common difference of an AP is always constant or variable?**

Ans Common difference of an *AP* is always constant.

Q.2 **Does the result obtain from the formulae, $S_n = \frac{n}{2}[2a + (n-1)d]$ and $S_n = \frac{n}{2}[a + l]$ are same?**

Ans Yes, results obtain from both formulae are same. We use these two formulae for different situations.

Q.3 **What is the formula of S_n in an AP, if a is the first term, l is the last term and n is the number of terms?**

Ans $S_n = \frac{n}{2}(a + l)$

Q.4 **What is the formula for a_n in S_n, if S_n is the sum of first n terms of an AP?**

Ans $a_n = S_n - S_{n-1}$

Q.5 **If we double each of the first n natural numbers, then what will be the sum of first n numbers?**

Ans The sum can be calculated by formula, $S_n = n(n+1)$.

$$\left[\because\ S_n = \frac{n(n+1)}{2} \text{ on doubling the numbers, sum} = 2 \times \frac{n(n+1)}{2} = n(n+1)\right]$$

Q.6 **If x, y and z are in an AP, then how would you represent y as of x and z?**

Ans Given, x, y and z are in AP.

$$\therefore \quad y = \frac{x+z}{2}$$

Q.7 **What will be the sum of first 20 natural numbers?**

Ans 210

Q.8 **What will be the sum of first ten multiples of 3?**

Ans 165

Activity 4

OBJECTIVE

To find the sum of first n odd natural numbers.

Prior Knowledge

1. Concept of odd natural numbers.
2. Concept of Arithmetic Progression (AP).
3. Series formed by consecutive odd n natural numbers.

Materials Required

1. Cardboard
2. Thermocol balls
3. Pins
4. White paper
5. Pencil
6. Geometry box
7. Adhesive

Theory

1. For concept of Arithmetic Progression (AP) see Activity 2.
2. From the series of odd natural numbers 1, 3, 5, 7, ..., it is clear that the difference between any two consecutive numbers is same, i.e. 2. So, it is an AP.

   nth term of AP, $T_n = a + (n-1)\,d$

   where, $a = 1$ and $d = 3 - 1 = 5 - 3 = 7 - 5 = 2$

   $\therefore \quad T_n = 1 + (n-1) \times 2$

   $= 1 + 2n - 2 = 2n - 1$

   So, the series can be written as 1, 3, 5, 7, ..., $(2n - 1)$.

   Sum of n terms of an AP, $S_n = \frac{n}{2}[2a + (n-1)\,d]$

   For the series, 1, 3, 5, 7, ..., n; $a = 1$ and $d = 2$

   $\therefore \quad S_n = \frac{n}{2}[2 \times 1 + (n-1)2]$

   $= \frac{n}{2}[2 + 2n - 2]$

   $= \frac{n}{2} \times 2n = n^2$

Procedure

1. Take a piece of cardboard of suitable size and paste a white paper on it.
2. Let us find the sum of first 10 odd natural numbers, i.e. 1, 3, 5, 7, ..., 10. So, draw a square of suitable size on it (10 cm× 10 cm).
3. Divide this square into unit squares (1 cm× 1 cm).

4. Fix a thermocol ball in each square with the help of a pin. (see Fig. 4.1)
5. Enclose (⌊) the balls as shown in the figure.

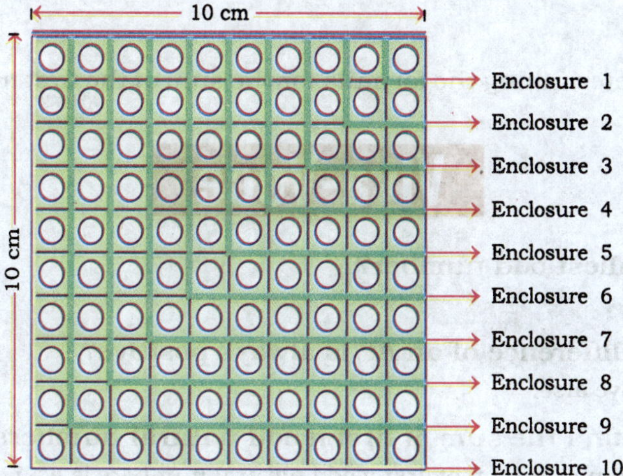

Fig. 4.1

Demonstration

Starting from the upper most right corner. (see Fig. 4.1)

The number of balls in first enclosure = $1 (= 1^2)$

The number of balls in first 2 enclosures = $1 + 3 = 4 (= 2^2)$

The number of balls in first 3 enclosures = $1 + 3 + 5 = 9 (= 3^2)$

The number of balls in first 4 enclosures = $1 + 3 + 5 + 7 = 16 (= 4^2)$

The number of balls in first 5 enclosures = $1 + 3 + 5 + 7 + 9 = 25 (= 5^2)$

So, the number of balls in first 10 enclosures = $1 + 3 + 5 + \dots + 19 = 100 (= 10^2)$

This gives the sum of first ten odd natural numbers.

This result can be generalised for the sum of first n odd natural numbers as

$$S_n = 1 + 3 + 5 + 7 + \dots + (2n - 1) = n^2 \qquad \text{...(i)}$$

Observations

On actual measurement, we observe that

On putting $n = 8$ in Eq. (i), we get S_n = ...

On putting $n = 9$ in Eq. (i), we get S_n = ...

On putting $n = 30$ in Eq. (i), we get S_n = ...

On putting $n = 50$ in Eq. (i), we get S_n = ...

On putting $n = 100$ in Eq. (i), we get S_n = ...

Result

We have found the sum of the first n odd natural numbers.

Application

The activity is useful in determining the formula for the sum of the first n odd natural numbers.

Viva-Voce

Q.1 What is the smallest odd number?

Ans 1

Q.2 Is the common difference of an AP is always positive?

Ans No, it can be negative also.

Q.3 How would you find the sum of first *n* odd natural numbers?

Ans The formula for finding the sum of first n odd natural numbers is n^2, i.e. $S_n = n^2$.

Q.4 Think about any two consecutive odd natural numbers. Is the difference between them is 2?

Ans Yes, the common difference between any two consecutive odd natural numbers is always 2.

Q.5 What will be the sum of first ten odd natural numbers?

Ans 100

Activity 5

OBJECTIVE

To find the sum of first n even natural numbers.

Prior Knowledge

1. Concept of even natural numbers.
2. Concept of Arithmetic Progression (AP).
3. Concept of series formed by consecutive even n natural numbers.

Materials Required

1. Cardboard
2. Thermocol balls
3. Pins
4. White paper
5. Pencil
6. Geometry box
7. Adhesive

Theory

1. For concept of Arithmetic Progression (AP) see Activity 2.
2. From the series of even natural numbers 2, 4, 6, 8, ..., it is clear that the difference between any two consecutive numbers are same, i.e. 2. So, it is an AP.

   nth term of an AP is

   $$T_n = a + (n-1)\,d$$

   Here, $a = 2$, $d = 4-2 = 6-4 = 8-6 = 2$

   $$\therefore \quad T_n = 2 + (n-1)\,2 = 2 + 2n - 2 = 2n$$

   So, the series can be written as 2, 4, 6, 8, ..., $2n$.

   We know that the sum of first n terms of a given arithmetic progression is

   $$S_n = \frac{n}{2}[2a + (n-1)\,d]$$

   For the series 2, 4, 6, 8, ..., $2n$; $a = 2$ and $d = 2$

   $$\therefore \quad S_n = \frac{n}{2}[2 \times 2 + (n-1) \times 2]$$

   $$= \frac{n}{2}[4 + 2n - 2] = \frac{2n}{2}(n+1) = n(n+1)$$

Procedure

1. Take a piece of cardboard of suitable size and paste a white paper on it.
2. Let us find the sum of first 10 even natural numbers, i.e. 2, 4, 6, ..., 20. So, draw a rectangle of suitable size on it (10 cm × 11 cm).
3. Divide this rectangle into unit squares (1 cm × 1 cm).
4. Fix a thermocol ball in each square using a pin as shown in Fig 5.1.

5. Enclose (⌡) the balls as shown in Fig 5.1.

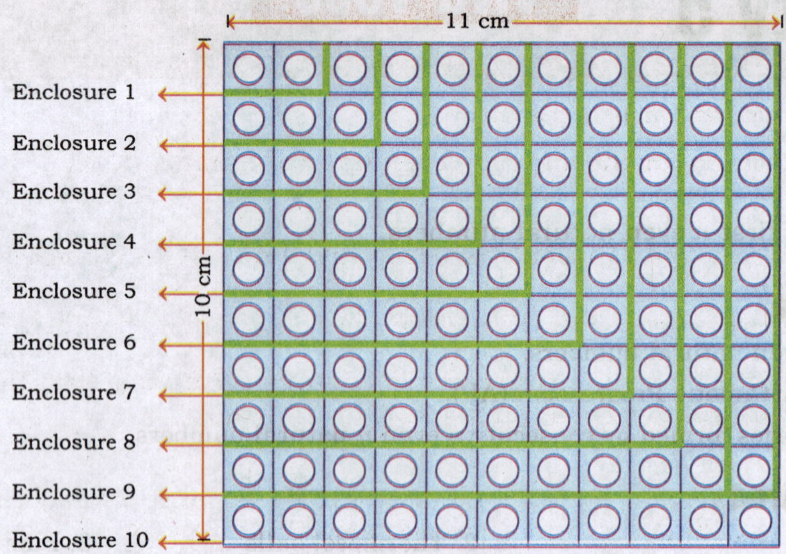

Fig. 5.1

Demonstration

Starting from the uppermost left corner. (see Fig. 5.1)

1. The number of balls in first enclosure = 2 (= 1 × 2)
2. The number of balls in first two enclosures = 2 + 4 = 6 (= 2 × 3)
3. The number of balls in first three enclosures = 2 + 4 + 6 = 12 (= 3 × 4)
4. The number of balls in first six enclosures = 2 + 4 + 6 + 8 + 10 + 12 = 42 (= 6 × 7)
5. The number of balls in first ten enclosures = 2 + 4 + 6 + 8 + ... + 20 = 110 (= 10 × 11)

   This gives the sum of first ten even natural numbers.

   This result can be generalised for the sum of first n even natural numbers, as

$$S_n = 2 + 4 + 6 + \ldots + 2n = n \times (n + 1) \quad \ldots(i)$$

Observation

On actual measurement, we observe that

On putting $n = 4$ in Eq. (i), S_n = ...

On putting $n = 6$ in Eq. (i), S_n = ...

On putting $n = 40$ in Eq. (i), S_n = ...

On putting $n = 70$ in Eq. (i), S_n = ...

On putting $n = 100$ in Eq. (i), S_n = ...

Result

We have found the sum of the first n even natural numbers.

Application

The formula $S_n = n(n + 1)$ is useful in finding out the sum of the first n even natural numbers.

Viva-Voce

Q.1 Write the *n*th even natural number.

Ans The *n*th even natural numbers is given by $2n$.

Q.2 Write the formula for the sum of *n* even natural numbers.

Ans $n(n + 1)$

Q.3 Think about any two consecutive even natural numbers. Is the difference between them is 2?

Ans Yes, the difference between any two consecutive even natural numbers is 2, i.e. $4 - 2 = 2$, $6 - 4 = 2$.

Q.4 The sum of first 10 natural numbers is equal to the sum of first five odd numbers and first five even numbers. (True/False)

Ans True

Q.5 Let the sum of first 10 even numbers be 110. If we multiply each number by *a*, then the new sum will be 110 *a*. (True/False)

Ans True

Q.6 If each term of an AP is divided by non-zero constant, then the new sequence will be in AP. (True/False)

Ans True

Q.7 What will be the sum of first ten even natural numbers?

Ans 110

Activity 6

OBJECTIVE

To establish a formula for the sum of first n terms of an arithmetic progression.

Prior Knowledge

1. Concept of AP.
2. Formula for sum of n terms of an AP.

Materials Required

1. Cardboard
2. Coloured drawing sheets
3. Adhesive
4. White paper
5. Cutter
6. Pencil
7. Geometry box

Theory

For concept of AP refer to Activity 2 and for formula for sum of n terms of an AP refer to Activity 3.

Procedure

1. Take a rectangular cardboard of suitable size and paste a white paper on it.
2. Draw a rectangle $ABCD$ of length $(2a + 9d)$ units and breadth 10 units.
3. Make some rectangular strips of equal length a units and breadth one unit and some strips of length d units and breadth 1 unit, using coloured drawing sheets. For measuring purpose take $a = 3$ units and $d = 2$ units
4. Arrange/paste these strips on the rectangle $ABCD$. (see Fig. 6.1).

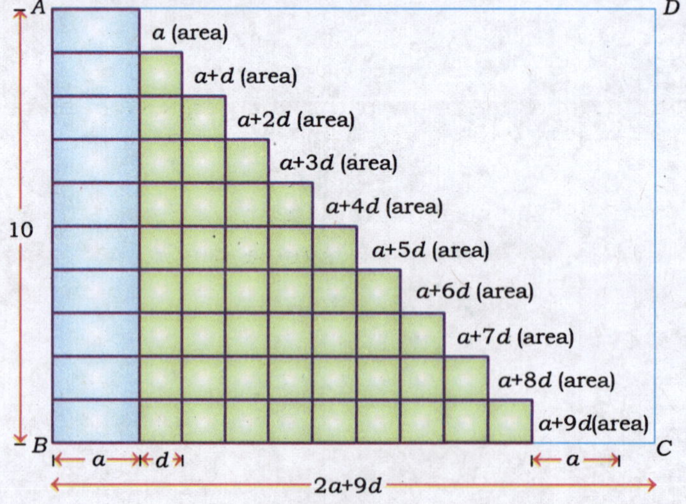

Fig. 6.1

Demonstration

1. The strips which are arranged look like a stair case.
2. The first stair is of length a units, the second stair is of length $a + d$ (units), third is of length $a + 2d$ units and so on and each is having breadth 1 unit.

   So, the areas (in sq units) of these strips are $a, a + d, a + 2d, \ldots, a + 9d$ respectively.

   [$\because$ area of rectangle = length $\times$ breadth, here in each case breadth is 1 unit]
3. This arrangements of strips are in a pattern $a, a + d, a + 2d, a + 3d, \ldots$

   which is an AP (difference between any two consecutive terms is same) with first term a and the common difference d.
4. The sum of the areas (in sq units) of these strips

   $$= a + (a + d) + (a + 2d) + \ldots + (a + 9d) = 10a + 45d \qquad \ldots(i)$$
5. Area of the design formed by the stair case $= \frac{1}{2}$ Area of rectangle $ABCD$

   $$= \frac{1}{2}(10)(2a + 9d)$$
   $$= 10a + 45d$$

   Which is the same as obtained in Eq. (i).

   This shows that the sum of first 10 terms of the AP $= \frac{1}{2}(10)(2a + 9d)$

   $$= \frac{1}{2}(10)[2a + (10 - 1)d]$$
6. This result can be further generalised to find the sum of first n terms of an AP, as

   $$S_n = \frac{n}{2}[2a + (n - 1)d]$$

Observation

On actual measurement, we observe that

$a = \ldots\ldots\ldots$, $d = \ldots\ldots\ldots$,

$n = \ldots\ldots\ldots$, $S_n = \ldots\ldots\ldots$

So, $S_n = \frac{n}{2}[2a + (n - 1)d]$

Result

A formula for the sum of first n terms of an arithmetic progression has been established.

Applications

This result may be used to find the sum of first n terms of the list of numbers like

1. $1^2, 2^2, 3^2, \ldots$ 2. $1^3, 2^3, 3^3, \ldots$ which is to be studied in Class XI.

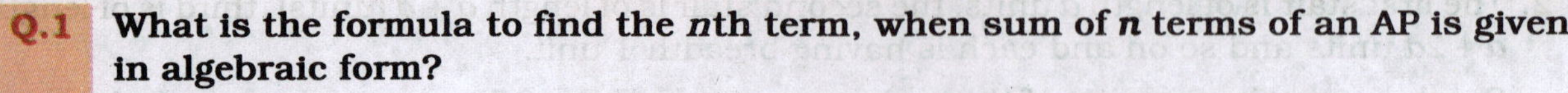

Viva-Voce

Q.1 What is the formula to find the nth term, when sum of n terms of an AP is given in algebraic form?

Ans $a_n = S_n - S_{n-1}$

Q.2 Is the sum of n terms of an AP be always negative?

Ans No

Q.3 What is the formula for the sum of n terms of an AP?

Ans Sum of n terms of an AP, $S_n = \frac{n}{2}[2a + (n-1)d]$.

Q.4 What is the formula for the sum of n terms of an AP, when last term is given?

Ans $S_n = \frac{n}{2}[a + l]$

Q.5 Let the sum of 10 terms of an AP series to be 30. If we increase each term be 1, then the sum of new series will be 40. (True/False)

Ans True

Activity 7

OBJECTIVE

To draw a system of similar squares using two intersecting strips with nails.

Prior Knowledge

1. Concept of similarity of figures.
2. Properties of square.

Materials Required

1. Two wooden strips of equal size (approx 1 cm wide and 30 cm long)
2. Adhesive
3. Hammer
4. Nails
5. Thread

Theory

1. Two figures having the same shape but not necessarily the same size, are called **similar figures**. If two figures are similar to each other, then one can be obtained from the other either by shrinking or by stretching without changing its shape.
2. A quadrilateral will be a square, if

   (i) its diagonals are equal. (ii) its diagonals bisect each other at 90°.

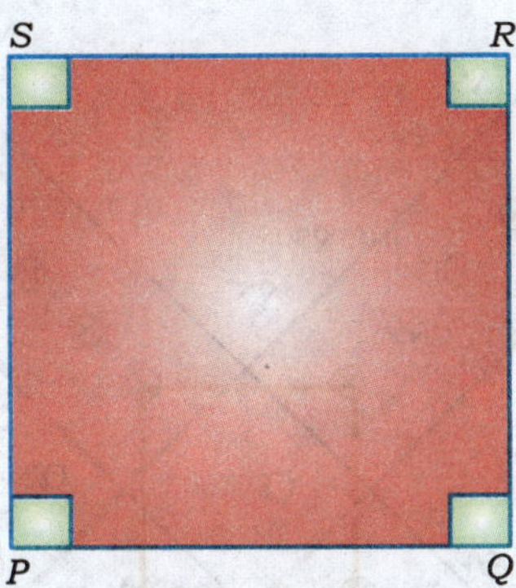

Fig. 7.1

In fig. 7.1, $PQ = QR = RS = PS$

and $\angle P = \angle Q = \angle R = \angle S = 90°$

Procedure

1. Take two wooden strips, say *PR* and *QS*.
2. Join both the strips, by using adhesive, such that they intersect each other at right angles, at the point *O*. (see Fig. 7.2)

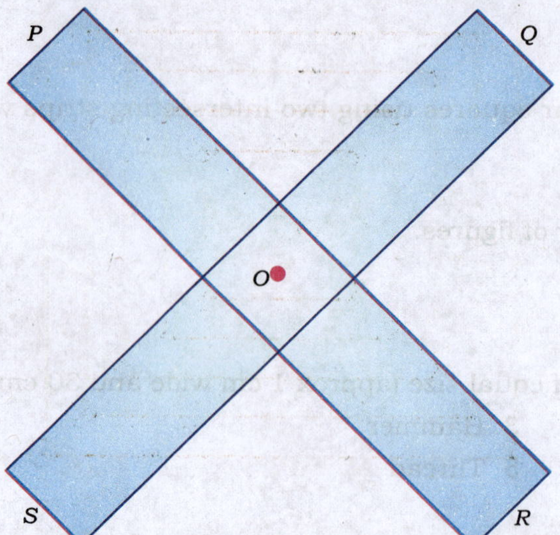

Fig. 7.2

3. Fix five nails at equal distances on each side of the strips (on each sides of *O*) and name them, say $P_1, P_2, \ldots P_5$; $R_1, R_2, \ldots, R_5$; $Q_1, Q_2, \ldots, Q_5$ and $S_1, S_2, \ldots, S_5$. (see Fig. 7.3)
4. Wind the thread around nails of subscript 1 ($P_1Q_1R_1S_1$) to get a square. (see Fig. 7.3)

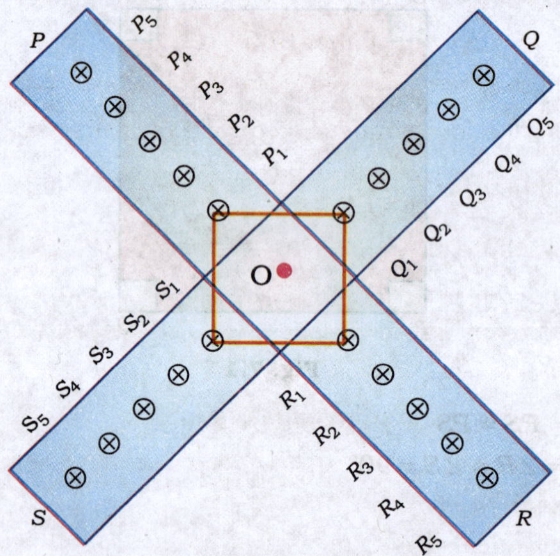

Fig. 7.3

5. Similarly, we wind the thread around nails of same subscript (see Fig. 7.4). We get, squares $P_1Q_1R_1S_1$, $P_2Q_2R_2S_2$, $P_3Q_3R_3S_3$, $P_4Q_4R_4S_4$ and $P_5Q_5R_5S_5$.

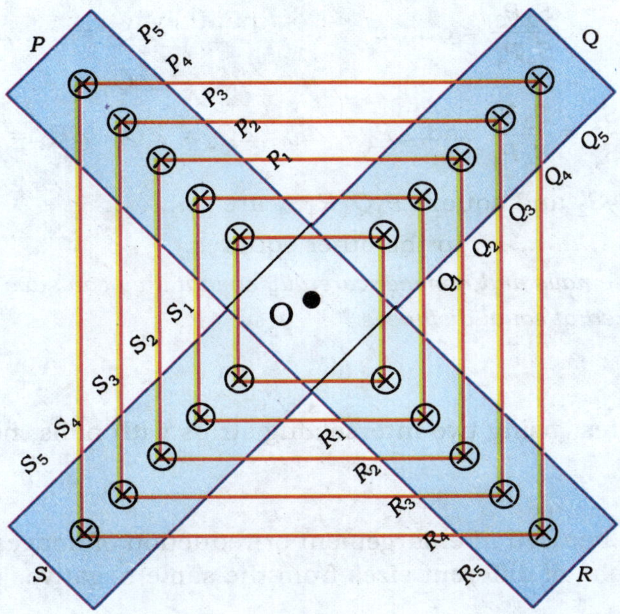

Fig. 7.4

Demonstration

1. On each side of the strips *PR* and *QS*, nails are positioned equidistant from each other, i.e.,

$$P_1P_2 = P_2P_3 = P_3P_4 = P_4P_5, \quad R_1R_2 = R_2R_3 = R_3R_4 = R_4R_5,$$
$$Q_1Q_2 = Q_2Q_3 = Q_3Q_4 = Q_4Q_5, \quad S_1S_2 = S_2S_3 = S_3S_4 = S_4S_5$$

2. On observing the quadrilateral $P_4Q_4R_4S_4$, we get, (see Fig. 7.4)

$$P_4O = OR_4 \text{ and } S_4O = OQ_4$$

i.e **diagonals** bisect each other. Therefore, $P_4Q_4R_4S_4$ is a parallelogram.

Moreover, $P_4R_4 = Q_4S_4$. i.e. diagonals are equal to each other.

In addition to this, P_4R_4 is perpendicular to Q_4S_4 (since, the strips are perpendicular to each other). Therefore, $P_4Q_4R_4S_4$ is a square.

Similarly, we can say that $(P_1Q_1R_1S_1)$, $(P_2Q_2R_2S_2)$, $(P_3Q_3R_3S_3)$ and $(P_5Q_5R_5S_5)$ are all squares.

3. Now, to show similarity of squares (see Fig. 7.4), measures P_1Q_1, P_2Q_2, P_3Q_3, P_4Q_4, P_5Q_5, Q_1R_1, Q_2R_2, Q_3R_3, Q_4R_4, Q_5R_5 and so on.

Also, find ratios of their corresponding sides, such as $\frac{P_1Q_1}{P_2Q_2}, \frac{P_2Q_2}{P_3Q_3}, \frac{Q_2R_2}{Q_3R_3}, \ldots$

Observation

By actual measurement, of sides and angles of squares $P_2Q_2R_2S_2$ and $P_4Q_4R_4S_4$, we get the following observations

P_2Q_2 = ...,	P_4Q_4 = ...,	$\angle P_2$ = ...,
Q_2R_2 = ...,	Q_4R_4 = ...,	$\angle R_2$ = ...,
R_2S_2 = ...,	R_4S_4 = ...,	$\angle P_4$ = ...,
S_2P_2 = ...,	S_4P_4 = ...,	$\angle R_4$ = ...,

$\frac{P_2Q_2}{P_4Q_4} = ...,$ $\frac{Q_2R_2}{Q_4R_4} = ...,$ $\angle Q_2 = ...,$

$\frac{R_2S_2}{R_4S_4} = ...,$ $\frac{S_2P_2}{S_4P_4} = ...$. $\angle S_2 = ...,$

$\angle Q_4 = ...,$

Here, $\frac{P_2Q_2}{P_4Q_4} = \frac{Q_2R_2}{Q_4R_4} = \frac{R_2S_2}{R_4S_4} = \frac{S_2P_2}{S_4P_4}$ and $\angle P_2 = \angle P_4$, $\angle Q_2 = \angle Q_4$, $\angle R_2 = \angle R_4$, $\angle S_2 = \angle S_4$.

Therefore, square $P_2Q_2R_2S_2$ and square $P_4Q_4R_4S_4$ are ....

Similarly, each square is .... to the other squares.

Note *(i) Students should use nails and hammer carefully so that they can save themselves from hurting.*

(ii) Nails should be fixed at equal distances.

Result

A system of similar squares, using two intersecting strips with nails, has been drawn.

Application

Concept of similarity can be used in enlargement or reduction of images like maps in Atlas and also in making photographs of different sizes from the same negative.

Viva-Voce

Q.1 What do you understand by the similar figures?

Ans Two figures having the same shape, (and not necessarily the same size) are called similar figures.

Q.2 What do you understand by the congruent figures?

Ans Two figures are said to be congruent, if they have the same shape and same size.

Q.3 What is the relation between congruency and similarity of figures?

Ans All congruent figures are similar to each other but all similar figures need not be to congruent.

Q.4 Which types of figure have same shape but not necessarily the same size?

Ans Similar figures

Q.5 Are square and rectangle similar? Justify your statement.

Ans No, in a square and a rectangle corresponding angles are always equal but their corresponding sides are not in the same ratio. So, a square and a rectangle are not similar.

Q.6 What is/are the condition(s) for similarity of two polygons?

Ans Conditions for similarity of two polygons are
(i) corresponding angles are equal.
(ii) lengths of their corresponding sides are proportional.

Q.7 Do you think, a circle and a square is similar to each other? Give reason for your answer.

Ans Since, they are of different shapes. So, they are not similar to each other.

Q.8 Are rhombus and square similar? Justify your statement.

Ans No, a rhombus and a square are not similar because their corresponding angles are not equal.

Q.9 Two polygons of the same number of sides are similar, if

(a) their corresponding sides are —— and

(b) their corresponding angles are ——.

Ans Proportional and equal.

Q.10 State the properties of square.

Ans
1. All sides are equal.
2. All angles are equal to 90°.
3. Diagonal are equal and bisect each other at 90°.

Activity 8

OBJECTIVE

To draw a system of similar triangles, using *Y*-shaped strips with nails.

Prior Knowledge

1. Concept of similarity of figures.
2. Criterion for similarity of two triangles.

Materials Required

1. Three wooden strips of equal size (approx 10 cm long and 1 cm wide)
2. Adhesive/Adhesive tape
3. Nails
4. Hammer
5. Thread

Theory

1. For concept of similarity of figures see Activity 7.
2. Two triangles are said to be similar, if
   (i) their corresponding angles are equal, **(by AAA similarity criterion)**.
   (ii) two angles of one triangle are respectively equal to the two angles of the other triangle,
   (by AA similarity criterion).
   (iii) sides of one triangle is proportional to (i.e. in the same ratio of) the sides of the other triangle, **(by SSS similarity criterion)**.
   (iv) one angle of a triangle is equal to one angle of another triangle and the sides including these angles are in the same ratio (proportional), **(by SAS similarity criterion)**.

Procedure

1. Take three wooden strips, say *P*, *Q*, *R* and cut one end of each strip.
2. Join three ends of each strip, by using adhesive/adhesive tape, such that they all lie in different directions. (see Fig. 8.1)

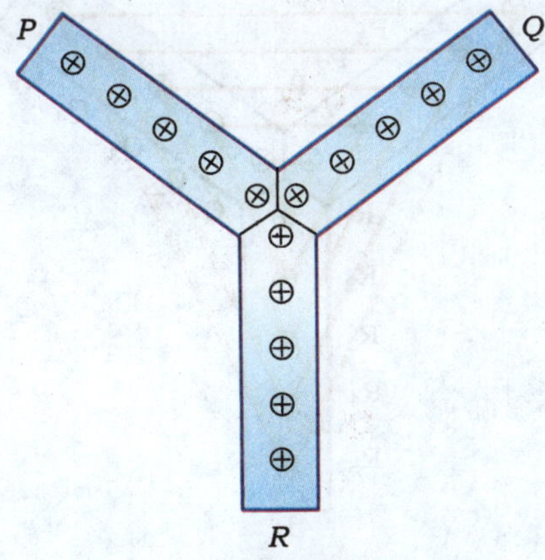

Fig 8.1

3. Fix five nails at same distance on each of the strips and name them $P_1, P_2, ..., P_5$; $Q_1, Q_2, ..., Q_5$ and $R_1, R_2, ..., R_5$ on strips P, Q and R, respectively. (see Fig. 8.2)

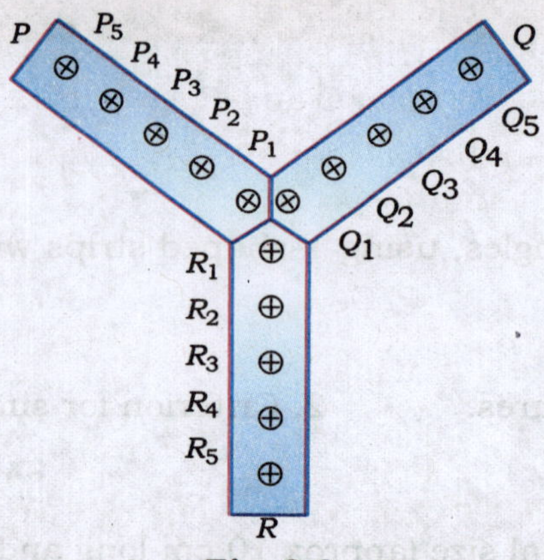

Fig. 8.2

4. On three respective strips, tie the thread around the nails of subscript 1 (P_1, Q_1, R_1). (see Fig. 8.3)

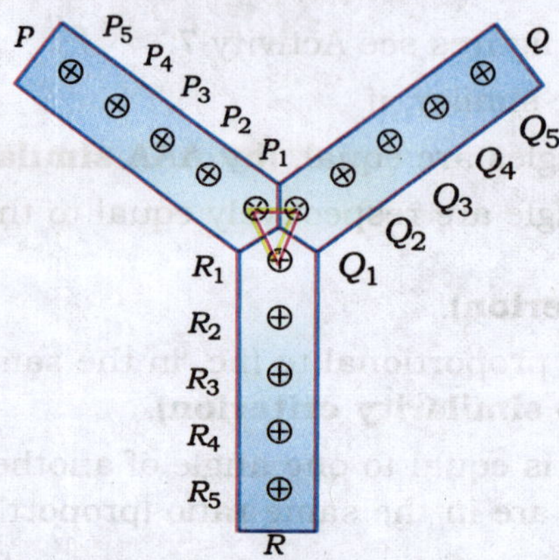

Fig. 8.3

5. Tie the thread around the nails of the same subscript on the respective strips for getting more such triangles. Thus, we get triangles $P_1Q_1R_1$, $P_2Q_2R_2$, $P_3Q_3R_3$, $P_4Q_4R_4$ and $P_5Q_5R_5$. (see Fig. 8.4)

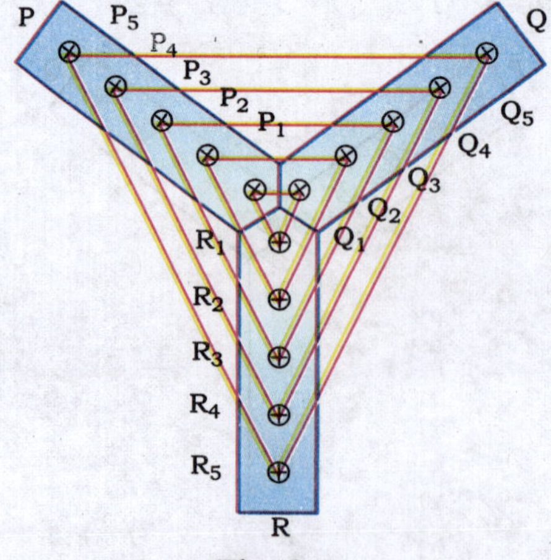

Fig. 8.4

Demonstration

1. Three wooden strips are fixed at some particular angles.
2. On each of the strips P, Q, R nails are positioned at equal distances such that $P_1P_2 = P_2P_3 = P_3P_4 = P_4P_5$ on strip P and similarly $Q_1Q_2 = Q_2Q_3 = Q_3Q_4 = Q_4Q_5$ and $R_1R_2 = R_2R_3 = R_3R_4 = R_4R_5$ on strip Q and R, respectively.
3. Now, take any two triangles say $P_1Q_1R_1$ and $P_5Q_5R_5$. Measure of sides P_1Q_1, P_5Q_5, P_1R_1, P_5R_5, R_1Q_1 and R_5Q_5.
4. Find the ratios $\frac{P_1Q_1}{P_5Q_5}$, $\frac{P_1R_1}{P_5R_5}$ and $\frac{R_1Q_1}{R_5Q_5}$
5. Observed that $\frac{P_1Q_1}{P_5Q_5} = \frac{P_1R_1}{P_5R_5} = \frac{R_1Q_1}{R_5Q_5}$.

   Thus, $\Delta P_1Q_1R_1 \sim P_5Q_5R_5$ [SSS similarity criterion]
6. It can be easily shown any two triangles formed on Y shaped strips are similar.

Observation

By actual measurement of sides of $\Delta P_1Q_1R_1$ and $\Delta P_5Q_5R_5$ we observe the following results

$P_1Q_1 =$ ...., $Q_1R_1 =$ ...., $R_1P_1 =$ ....,

$P_5Q_5 =$ ...., $Q_5R_5 =$ ...., $R_5P_5 =$ ....,

$\frac{P_1Q_1}{P_5Q_5} =$ ...., $\frac{Q_1R_1}{Q_5R_5} =$ ...., $\frac{R_1P_1}{R_5P_5} =$ ....

Here, $\frac{P_1Q_1}{P_5Q_5} = \frac{Q_1R_1}{Q_5R_5} = \frac{R_1P_1}{R_5P_5}$

Therefore, $\Delta P_1Q_1R_1$ and $\Delta P_5Q_5R_5$ are ....

Note *By tying a thread at suitable nails, we can obtain non-equilateral similar triangles also.*

Result

We have drawn a system of similar triangles, using Y-shaped strips with nails.

Applications

1. By using this concept, we can find the length of the shadow of pole in sunlight and height of a pole.
2. Using the concept of similarity, unknown dimensions of an object can be determined using a similar object with known dimensions.

Viva-Voce

Q.1 Define SSS similarity criterion?

Ans If in two triangles, corresponding sides are in the same ratio, then their corresponding angles are equal and hence the triangles are similar.

Q.2 Define AA similarity criterion.

Ans If in two triangles, two angles of one triangle are respectively equal to the two angles of the other triangle, then the two triangles are similar.

Q.3 If $\Delta ABC \sim \Delta MLP$, then what will be the corresponding ratio of the sides?

Ans If, $\Delta ABC \sim \Delta MLP$, then $\frac{AB}{ML} = \frac{BC}{LP} = \frac{CA}{PM}$

Q.4 If in ΔABC and ΔPRQ, $\frac{AC}{RQ} = \frac{BA}{QP} = \frac{BC}{RP}$, then how would you represent the pair of similar triangles in their symbolic form?

Ans $\Delta ACB \sim \Delta QRP$

Q.5 It is given that $\Delta FED \sim \Delta STU$. Is it true to say that $\frac{DE}{ST} = \frac{EF}{TU}$? Why?

Ans No, because the correct correspondence is $F \leftrightarrow S$, $E \leftrightarrow T$, $D \leftrightarrow U$. With this correspondence, $\frac{EF}{ST} = \frac{DE}{TU}$.

Q.6 If in ΔABC and ΔDEF, $\frac{AB}{DE} = \frac{BC}{FD}$ follows SAS criterion, then on what basis, we can say that they are similar?

Ans Since, we have $\frac{AB}{DE} = \frac{BC}{FD}$

$\therefore$ On having $\angle B = \angle D$, we can say that they will be similar and will follow SAS criterion.

Q.7 State whether the following triangles are similar or not. Give reason(s).

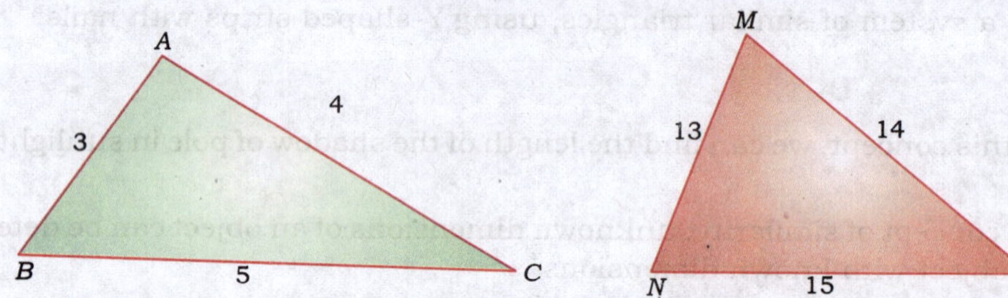

Ans No, given triangles are not similar as their corresponding sides are not proportional.

Q.8 "If in two triangles, one angle of a triangle is equal to one angle of another triangle and the sides including these angles, are in the same proportion." What can you conclude from the given information?

Ans We can conclude from the given information that both the triangles are similar to each other and follows SAS similarity criterion. So, the corresponding angles of both the triangles are equal and their corresponding sides are also in the same proportion.

Activity 9

OBJECTIVE

To verify Basic Proportionality Theorem (Thales theorem).

Prior Knowledge

Statement of Basic Proportionality Theorem (Thales theorem).

Materials Required

1. Two wooden strips of equal size (approx 1 cm wide and 30 cm long)
2. Cutter
3. Adhesive
4. Hammer
5. Nails
6. Hardboard
7. White paper
8. Pulleys
9. Thread
10. Scale
11. Screws
12. Coloured glazed papers.

Theory

According to Thales theorem, if a line is drawn parallel to one side of a triangle to intersect the other two sides at distinct points, then the other two sides are divided in the same ratio.

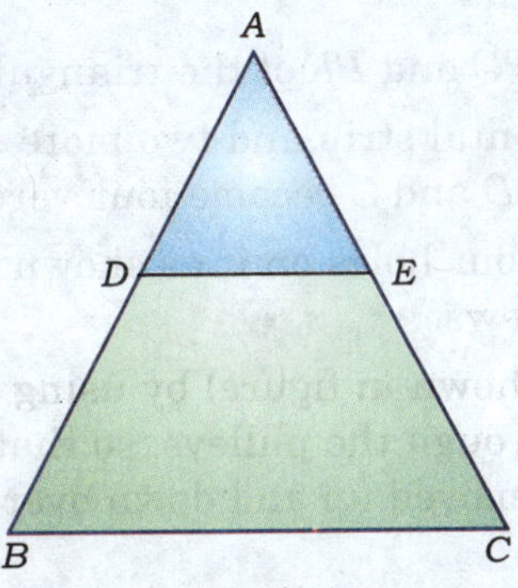

Fig. 9.1

In ΔABC, if $DE \parallel BC$, then according to Basic proportionality theorem, $\frac{AD}{DB} = \frac{AE}{EC}$.

Procedure

1. Cut a piece of hardboard of suitable size and paste a white paper on it.
2. Take two thin wooden strips with markings 1, 2, 3, ... at equal distances and fix them vertically on the two ends of the horizontal strip as shown in Fig. 9.2 and name them *AC* and *BD*.

3. From hardboard, cut a triangular piece *PQR* (thickness should be negligible) and paste coloured glazed paper on it and place it between the parallel strips *AC* and *BD* such that its base *QR* is parallel to the horizontal strip *AB* as shown in Fig. 9.2.

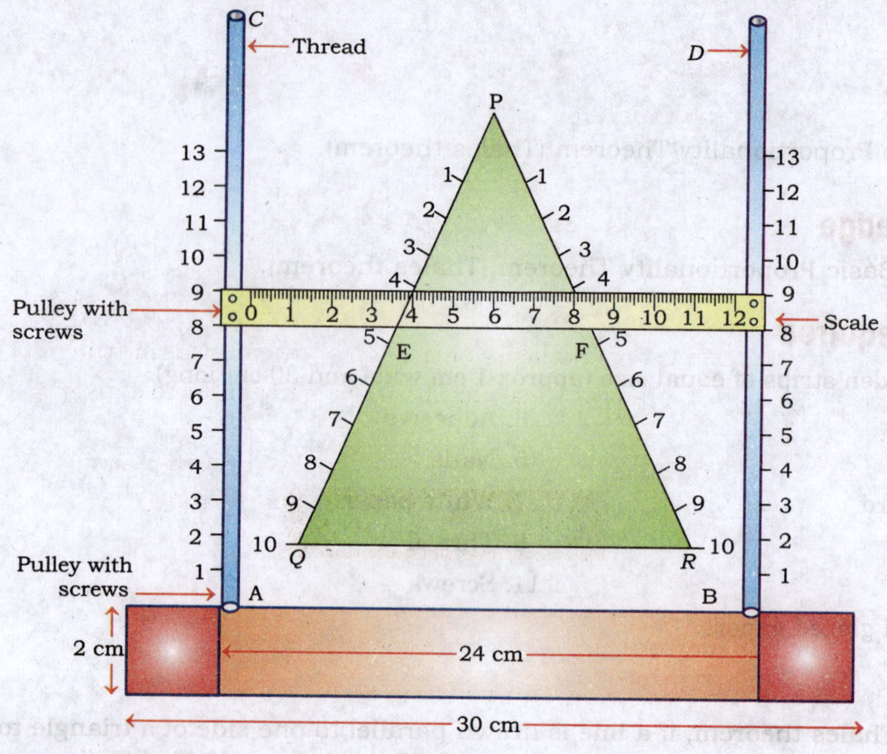

Fig. 9.2

4. Graduate the other two sides, *PQ* and *PR* of the triangular piece as shown in Fig. 9.2.
5. Put the screws along the horizontal strip and two more screws on the top of the board at the points *C* and *D*, such that *A*, *B*, *D* and *C* become four vertices of a rectangle.
6. Take a ruler (scale) and make four holes on it as shown in the figure and fix four pulleys at these holes with the help of screws.
7. Fix the scale on the board (as shown in figure) by using the thread tied to nails fixed at points *A*, *B*, *C* and *D* passing through the pulleys, so that the scale slides parallel to the horizontal strip *AB* and can be moved up and down over the triangular piece freely.

Demonstration

Set the scale on vertical strips parallel to the base *QR* of ΔPQR, say at points *E* and *F*. Measure the distance *PE* and *EQ* and also measure the distance *PF* and *FR*.

Here, $\frac{PE}{EQ} = \frac{PF}{FR}$. So, it verifies the Basic Proportionality Theorem.

Repeat the activity as stated above, slide the scale up and down parallel to the base of the ΔPQR and verify the Thales theorem for different positions of the scale.

Observation

By actual measurement, we observe the following results

$PE = ...,$ $PF = ...,$ $EQ = ...,$ $FR = ...,$

$\frac{PE}{EQ} = ...,$ $\frac{PF}{FR} = ...$.

Thus, $\frac{PE}{EQ} = \frac{PF}{FR}$. It verifies the theorem.

Result

Basic Proportionality Theorem (Thales theorem) has been verified.

Applications

1. To establish various criteria of similarity of triangles, we can use this theorem.
2. This theorem can also be used for constructing a polygon similar to a given polygon with a given scale factor.

Q.1 Give two examples of non-similar figures.

Ans (i) A triangle and a quadrilateral. (ii) A square and a rhombus.

Q.2 What is the another name of Thales theorem?

Ans Basic Proportionality Theorem

Q.3 Name the mathematician after whom the, BPT has another name.

Ans Thales

Q.4 State Thales theorem.

Ans If a line is drawn parallel to one side of a triangle, intersecting the other two sides, then it divides the two sides in the same ratio.

Q.5 What is the full form of BPT?

Ans Basic Proportionality Theorem

Q.6 If a line divides any two sides of a triangle in the same ratio, then the line is .... to the third side.

Ans Parallel

Q.7 A line is drawn parallel to one side of a triangle to intersect the other two sides in distinct points, does the other two sides are divided in different ratio?

Ans No, according to the Thales theorem, it will divide the other two sides in the same ratio.

Q.8 State converse of Basic Proportionality Theorem.

Ans If a line divides any two sides of a triangle in the same ratio, then the line must be parallel to the third side.

Activity 10

OBJECTIVE

To establish the criteria for similarity of two triangles.

Prior Knowledge

1. Concept of similarity of figures.
2. Condition for two triangles to be similar.
3. Basic Proportionality Theorem (BPT).

Materials Required

1. Coloured papers/Chart papers
2. Adhesive
3. Geometry box
4. Scissors

Theory

1. For concept of similarity of two figures see Activity 7.
2. For condition of two triangles to be similar see Activity 8.
3. For BPT see Activity 9.

Note *Converse of BPT is also true, i.e. if a line divides any two sides of triangles in the same ratio, then the line must be parallel to third side.*

Procedure

Case I

1. Take two different coloured papers/chart papers and cut out two triangles, ΔABC and ΔPQR having equal corresponding angles. (see Fig. 10.1 and Fig 10.2)

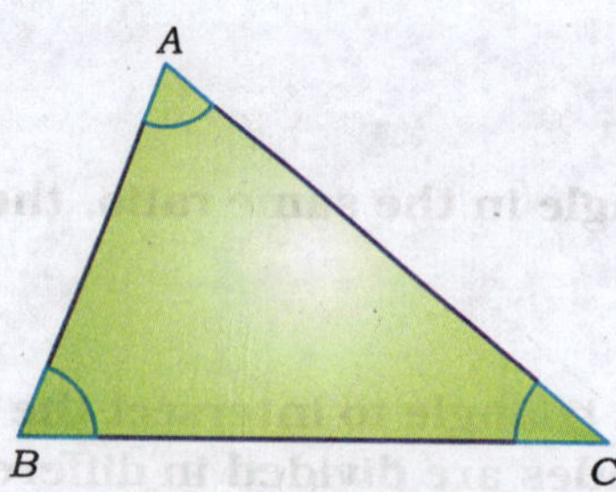

Fig. 10.1

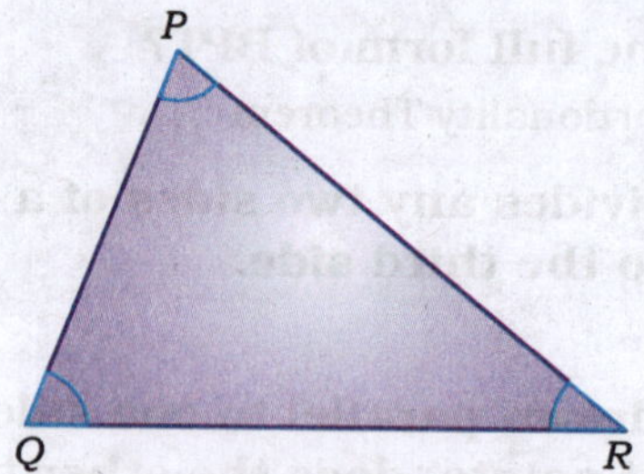

Fig. 10.2

2. In ΔABC and ΔPQR, $\angle A = \angle P$, $\angle B = \angle Q$ and $\angle C = \angle R$.

3. Place ΔABC on ΔPQR, such that vertex A falls on vertex P and side AB falls along side PQ (side AC falls along side PR) as shown in Fig. 10.3.

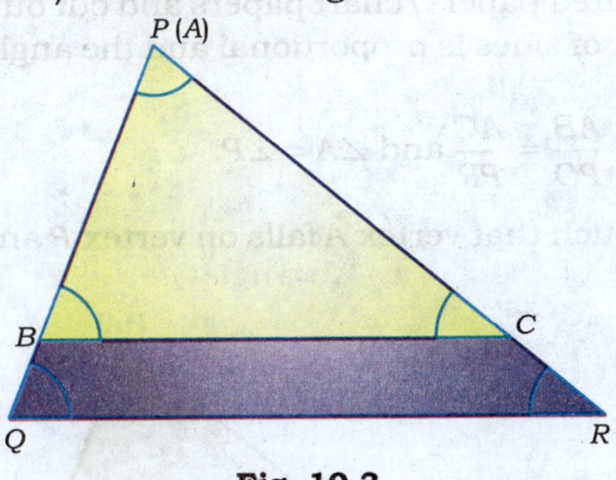

Fig. 10.3

Case II

1. Place the ΔABC on ΔPQR such that vertex B falls on vertex Q and side BA falls along side QP (side BC falls along side QR) as shown in Fig. 10.4.

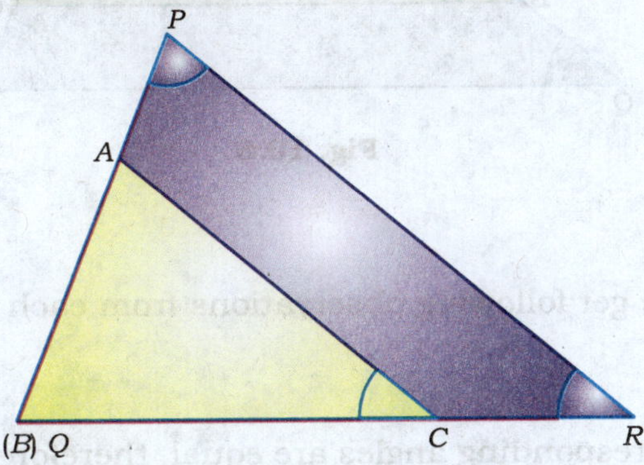

Fig. 10.4

Case III

1. Take two different coloured papers/chart papers and cut out two triangles, ΔABC and ΔPQR, with their corresponding sides proportional.

   i.e. $$\frac{AB}{PQ} = \frac{BC}{QR} = \frac{AC}{PR}$$

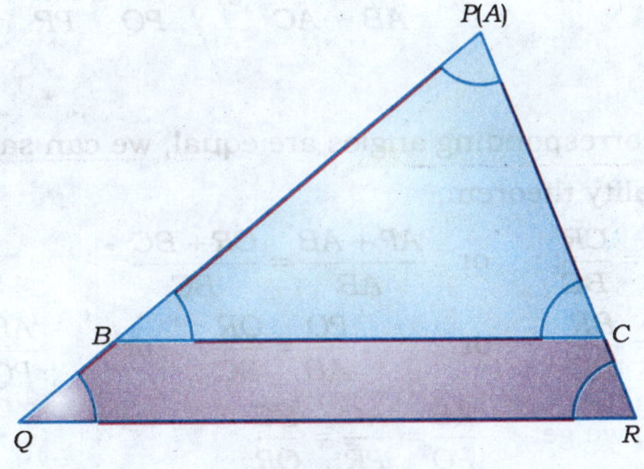

Fig. 10.5

2. Place the ΔABC on ΔPQR such that vertex A falls on vertex P and side AB falls along side PQ. Observe that side AC falls along side PR. (see Fig. 10.5)

Case IV

1. Take two different coloured papers/chart papers and cut out two triangles, ΔABC and ΔPQR such that their one pair of sides is proportional and the angles included between the pair of sides are equal.

   i.e. in ΔABC and ΔPQR, $\frac{AB}{PQ} = \frac{AC}{PR}$ and $\angle A = \angle P$.

2. Place ΔABC on ΔPQR, such that vertex A falls on vertex P and side AB falls along side PQ as shown in Fig. 10.6.

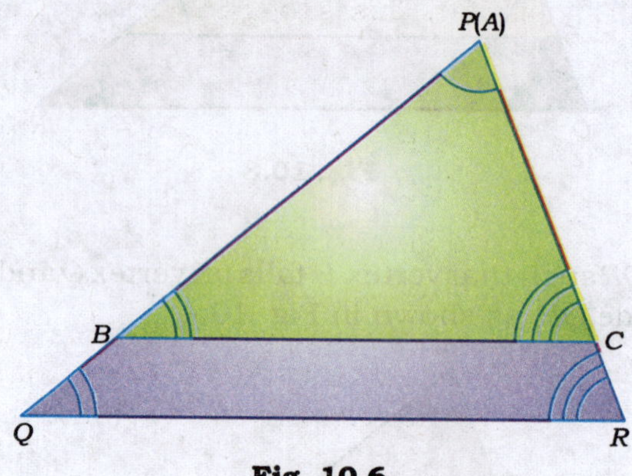

Fig. 10.6

Demonstration

By actual measurement, we get following observations from each of the given case.

Case I

1. Since, in Fig. 10.3 corresponding angles are equal, therefore we can say that $BC \parallel QR$.
2. By BPT

$$\frac{PB}{BQ} = \frac{PC}{CR} \quad \text{or} \quad \frac{AB}{BQ} = \frac{AC}{CR}$$

$$\text{or} \quad \frac{BQ}{AB} = \frac{CR}{AC} \quad \text{or} \quad \frac{BQ + AB}{AB} = \frac{CR + AC}{AC} \qquad \text{[adding 1 both sides]}$$

$$\text{or} \quad \frac{AQ}{AB} = \frac{AR}{AC} \quad \text{or} \quad \frac{PQ}{AB} = \frac{PR}{AC} \quad \text{or} \quad \frac{AB}{PQ} = \frac{AC}{PR} \qquad \text{...(i)}$$

Case II

1. Since, in Fig. 10.4, corresponding angles are equal, we can say that $AC \parallel PR$.
2. By Basic Proportionality theorem,

$$\frac{AP}{AB} = \frac{CR}{BC}; \quad \text{or} \quad \frac{AP + AB}{AB} = \frac{CR + BC}{BC} \qquad \text{[on adding 1 both sides]}$$

$$\text{or} \quad \frac{BP}{AB} = \frac{BR}{BC} \quad \text{or} \quad \frac{PQ}{AB} = \frac{QR}{BC} \quad \text{or} \quad \frac{AB}{PQ} = \frac{BC}{QR} \qquad \text{...(ii)}$$

From Eqs. (i) and (ii), we get $\frac{AB}{PQ} = \frac{AC}{PR} = \frac{BC}{QR}$

Thus, from **Case I and II,** we find that when the corresponding angles of two triangles are equal, then their corresponding sides are proportional. Hence, the two triangles are similar. This is AAA criterion for similarity of two triangles.

Case III

1. In Fig. 10.5, $\frac{AB}{PQ} = \frac{AC}{PR}$. This gives $\frac{AB}{BQ} = \frac{AC}{CR}$.

   So, we can say that $BC \parallel QR$ (by converse of Basic Proportionality theorem), i.e. $\angle B = \angle Q$ and $\angle C = \angle R$. Also, $\angle A = \angle P$. So, the corresponding angles of two triangles are equal.

   Thus, we see that when the corresponding sides of two triangles are proportional, their corresponding angles are equal.

   Hence, the two triangles are similar. This is the SSS criterion for similarity of two triangles.

Case IV

1. In Fig. 10.6, $\frac{AB}{PQ} = \frac{AC}{PR}$. This gives $\frac{AB}{BQ} = \frac{AC}{CR}$.

   So, $BC \parallel QR$ (by converse of Basic Proportionality theorem)

   Therefore, $\angle B = \angle Q$ and $\angle C = \angle R$.

   From this demonstration, we find that when two sides of one triangle are proportional to two sides of another triangle and the angles included between the two pairs of sides are equal, then corresponding angles of two triangles are equal. This is the SAS criterion for similarity of two triangles.

Observation

By actual measurement, we get

From *Case* I *and* II, by actual measurement, we observe that

$\angle A =$ ...., $\angle P =$ ...., $\angle B =$ ...., $\angle Q =$ ...., $\angle C =$ ...., $\angle R =$ ....

$\frac{AB}{PQ} =$ ...., $\frac{BC}{QR} =$ ...., $\frac{AC}{PR} =$ ....

Thus, corresponding angles of two triangles are ...., and their corresponding sides are ......

Hence, the triangles are ....

From *Case* III, by actual measurement, we observe that $\frac{AB}{PQ} =$ ...., $\frac{BC}{QR} =$ ...., $\frac{AC}{PR} =$ ....,

$\angle A =$ ...., $\angle B =$ ...., $\angle C =$ ...., $\angle P =$ ...., $\angle Q =$ ...., $\angle R =$ ....

Thus, the corresponding sides of two triangles are ...., and their corresponding angles are ....

Hence, the triangles are ....

From *Case* IV, by actual measurement, we observe that

$\frac{AB}{PQ} =$ ...., $\frac{AC}{PR} =$ ....,

$\angle A =$ ...., $\angle P =$ ...., $\angle B =$ ...., $\angle Q =$ ...., $\angle C =$ ...., $\angle R =$ ....

Thus, two sides of one triangle are .... to the two sides of other triangles and angles included between them are .... Hence, the triangles are ......

Result

Criteria for similarity of two triangles has been established.

Application

The concept of similarity is used to enlarge and reduce the images or pictures of objects.

Viva-Voce

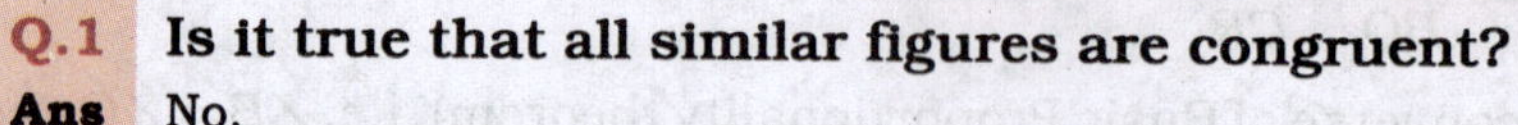

Q.1 Is it true that all similar figures are congruent?

Ans No.

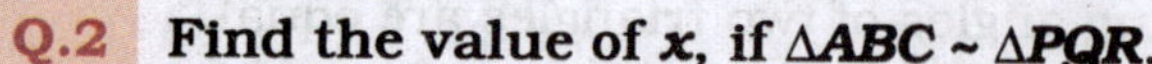

Q.2 Find the value of x, if $\Delta ABC \sim \Delta PQR$.

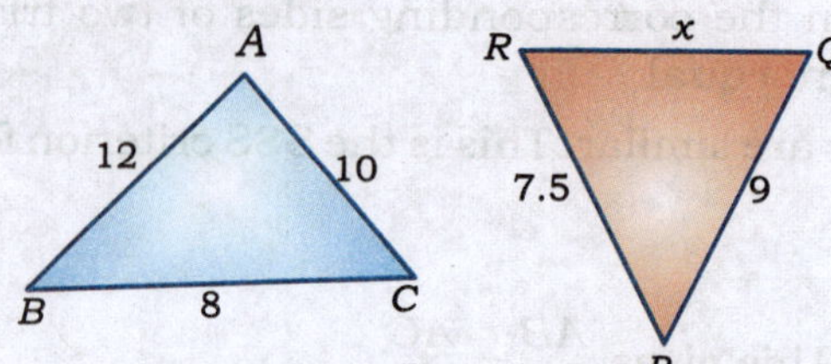

Ans $x = 6$

Q.3 'Any two congruent figures are similar'. Is this statement true? Justify your answer.

Ans Yes, two congruent figures are similar to each other. For example, two congruent squares have their sides equal, i.e. proportional to each other as well as all the corresponding angles are equal to each other.

Q.4 'Any two similar figures are congruent.' Is this statement true? Justify your answer.

Ans No, in similar figures, their corresponding angles are equal while their corresponding sides are proportional, not equal to each other. So, two similar figures are not necessarily congruent to each other. Hence, given statement is false.

Q.5 Give two examples of pair of similar figures.

Ans Two examples are

(i) any two equilateral triangles. (ii) any two regular pentagons.

Q.6 If $\Delta PQR \sim \Delta ABC$, then what can you conclude from the given information?

Ans We can conclude that $\frac{PQ}{AB} = \frac{QR}{BC} = \frac{RP}{CA}$ and $\angle P = \angle A$, $\angle Q = \angle B$ and $\angle R = \angle C$.

Q.7 'All circles are similar'. Justify this statement.

Ans All circles are similar because geometric figures which have same shape but different sizes are known as similar figures.

Q.8 'Any two squares are congruent.' Is this statement correct? If not, then rewrite it.

Ans Any two squares are congruent, is not a correct statement. It can be rewritten as 'Any two squares are similar'.

Q.9 'Two triangles are similar, if their corresponding angles are equal'. Is this statement valid? Give reason for your answer.

Ans We know that, two triangles are similar, if either their corresponding angles are equal or corresponding sides are proportional. So, the given statement is valid.

Q.10 If a triangle is similar to another triangle and this second triangle is similar to a third triangle, then what can you conclude about the first and third triangles?

Ans First triangle is also similar to the third triangle.

Activity 11

OBJECTIVE

To verify the distance formula by graphical method.

Prior Knowledge

1. Basic concepts of coordinate geometry.
2. Distance formula in coordinate geometry.

Materials Required

1. Cardboard
2. Chart paper
3. Graph paper
4. Adhesive
5. Pen/Pencil
6. Geometry box

Theory

1. **Basic Concept of Coordinate Geometry**

   (i) **Cartesian System** The position of any object lying in a plane can be represented with the help of two perpendicular lines. The system used to describe the position of a point in a plane, is called cartesian system.

   The point of intersection of these lines is called **origin** and it is denoted by *O*. In other words, the point from which distances are marked is called origin. The horizontal line *XOX′* is called **X-axis** and vertical line *YOY′* is called ***Y*-axis.**

   Directions *OX* and *OY* are called the **positive directions** of *X*-axis and *Y*-axis, respectively. Similarly, directions *OX′* and *OY′* are called the **negative directions** of *X*-axis and *Y*-axis, respectively. (see Fig. 11.1)

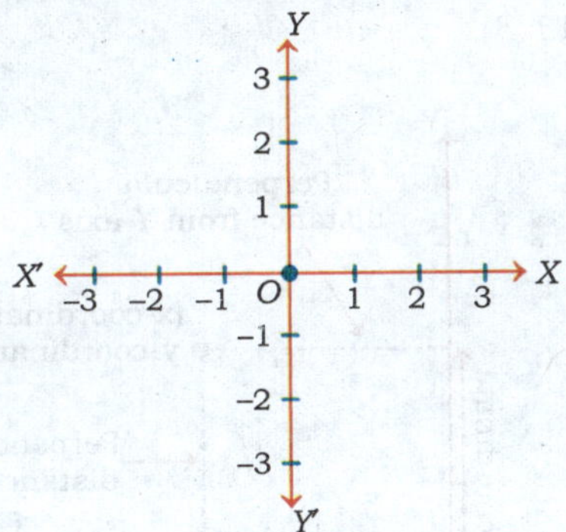

Fig. 11.1

(ii) **Quadrant** The intersection of X-axis and Y-axis divide the plane into four parts. These four parts are called quadrants. (see fig. 11.2)

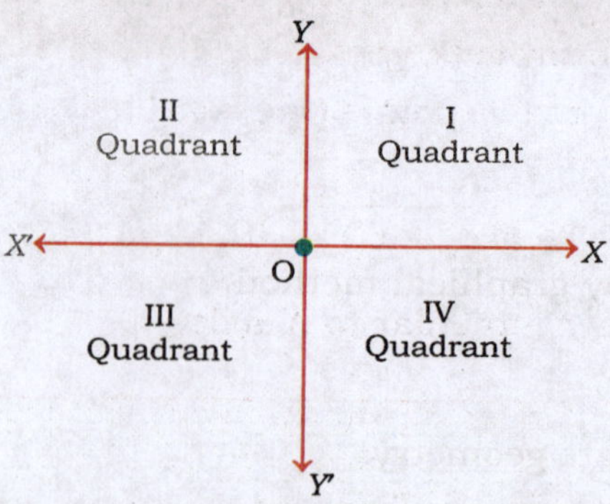

Fig. 11.2

(a) XOY is called the Ist quadrant.

(b) $X'OY$ is called the IInd quadrant.

(c) $X'OY'$ is called the IIIrd quadrant.

(d) XOY' is called the IVth quadrant.

(iii) **Coordinates of a Point in Cartesian Plane** To locate a point in the cartesian plane, its perpendicular distances from X-axis and Y-axis are required, these distances are called **coordinates** of the point. Each point in cartesian plane has two coordinates, i.e. x-coordinate and y-coordinate.

(a) The ***x*-coordinate** of a point is the perpendicular distance from the Y-axis measured along the X-axis (positive along the positive direction of the X-axis and negative along the negative direction of X-axis). The x-coordinate is also called the **abscissa.** (see fig. 11.3)

(b) The ***y*-coordinate** of a point is the perpendicular distance from the X-axis measured along the Y-axis (positive along the positive direction of the Y-axis and negative along the negative direction of Y-axis). The y-coordinate is also called the **ordinate**. (see fig. 11.3)

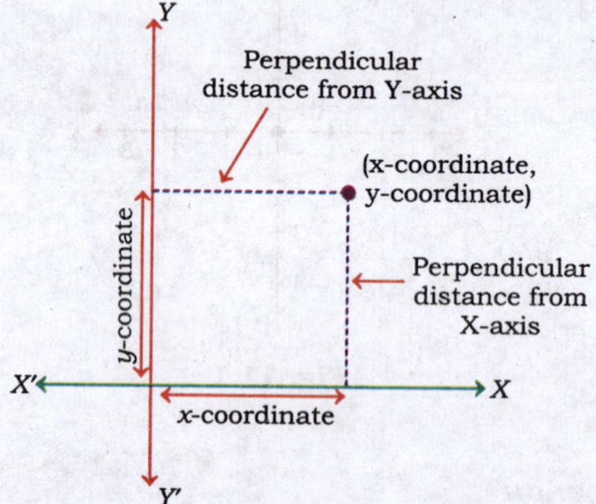

Fig. 11.3

x-coordinate and y-coordinate taken together are called **cartesian coordinates** or **coordinates** of a point and denoted by (x, y).

Here, (x, y) is called an **order pair**. The order of x and y is important in (x, y). Position of (y, x) will be different from (x, y).

2. Let $P(x_1, y_1)$ and $Q(x_2, y_2)$ be two points (see Fig. 11.4). Then the distance between P and Q is

$$PQ = \sqrt{(x_2 - x_1)^2 + (y_2 - y_1)^2}$$

Proof Draw PR and QS perpendicular to X-axis.

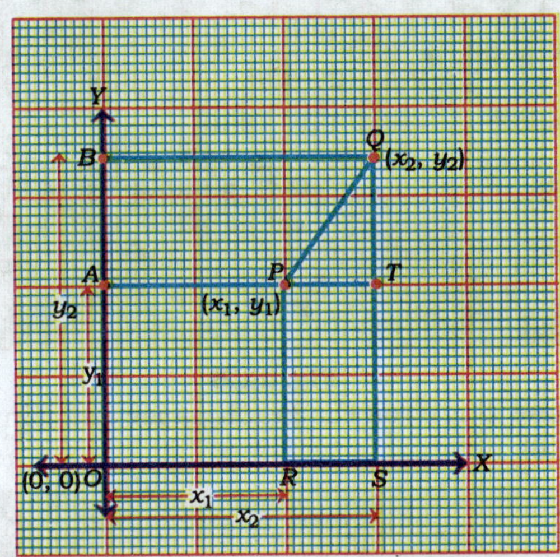

Fig. 11.4

A perpendicular drawn from P on QS to meet it at the point T.

Where, $OR = x_1, OS = x_2$

So, $RS = x_2 - x_1 = PT$

Also, $SQ = y_2, ST = PR = y_1$

So, $QT = y_2 - y_1$

Now, in right angled ΔPTQ, applying Pythagoras theorem, we get

$$PQ^2 = PT^2 + QT^2$$

$$= (x_2 - x_1)^2 + (y_2 - y_1)^2$$

Therefore, $$PQ = \sqrt{(x_2 - x_1)^2 + (y_2 - y_1)^2}$$

So, the distance between the points $P(x_1, y_1)$ and $Q(x_2, y_2)$ is

$$PQ = \sqrt{(x_2 - x_1)^2 + (y_2 - y_1)^2},$$

which is called **distance formula**.

Procedure

1. Paste a chart paper on a cardboard of suitable size.
2. Paste the graph paper on the chart paper.
3. Draw the axes $X'OX$ and $Y'OY$ on the graph paper. (see Fig. 11.5)

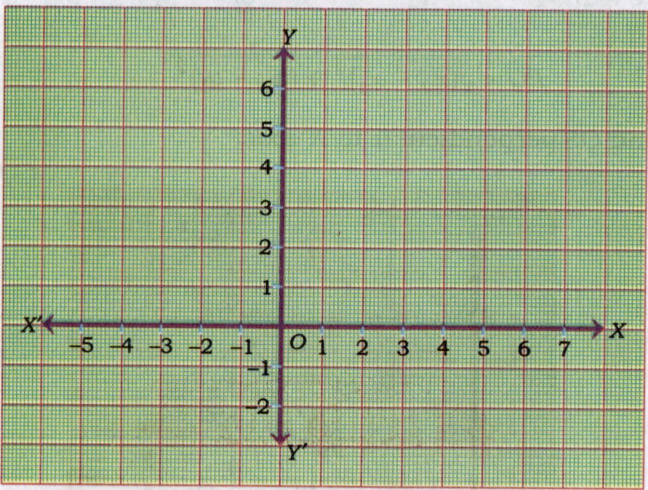

Fig. 11.5

4. Take two points $A(a, b)$ and $B(c, d)$ on the graph paper and join them so that a line segment AB is made. (see Fig. 11.6)

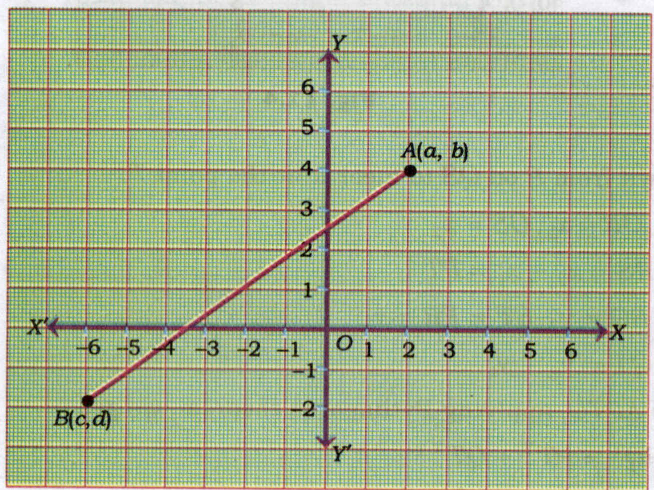

Fig. 11.6

Demonstration

1. Find the distance AB, using distance formula.
2. Measure the distance between the two points A and B, using a ruler.
3. The distance calculated by the distance formula and the distance measured by the ruler are same.

Observations

1. Coordinates of point *A* are ....
2. Coordinates of point *B* are ....
3. Distance *AB*, using distance formula .... units.
4. Actual distance *AB* measured by ruler, is .... units.
5. The distance calculated in observation 3 and actual distance measured in observation 4 are ....

Result

Distance formula by graphical method has been verified.

Application

Distance formula is used in proving a number of results in geometry.

Viva-Voce

Q.1 **What is the distance of the point (5, 9) from *X*-axis?**
Ans 9 units

Q.2 **What will be the distance of the point (3, 4) from *Y*-axis?**
Ans 3 units

Q.3 **Let $P(x_1, y_1)$ and $Q(x_2, y_2)$ be two points, what is the distance between these two points?**
Ans The distance between *P* and *Q* is $\sqrt{(x_2 - x_1)^2 + (y_2 - y_1)^2}$ units.

Q.4 **What will be the distance of a point $Q(a, b)$ from the origin?**
Ans $\sqrt{a^2 + b^2}$ units

Q.5 **Suppose *A* and *B* are two fixed points in a plane. If we shift the origin in another point, then the distance between *A* and *B* will remain same. (True/False)**
Ans True

Q.6 **Suppose a point *P* lies on *X*-axis, at a distance of 2 units from the origin in the positive direction of *X* – axis. Then, what are the coordinates of *P*?**
Ans. (2, 0)

Q.7 **What is the distance between the points (3, 0) and (0, 3)?**
Ans $\sqrt{18} = 3\sqrt{2}$ units

Q.8 **What is the distance of (4, 3) from origin?**
Ans 5 units

Activity 12

OBJECTIVE

To verify section formula by graphical method.

Prior Knowledge

1. Basic knowledge of coordinate geometry.
2. Section formula in coordinate geometry.

Materials Required

1. Cardboard
2. Graph paper
3. Pen/Pencil
4. Geometry box
5. Chart paper
6. Adhesive

Theory

1. For basic concept of coordinate geometry see Activity 11.
2. **Section Formula** The coordinates of a point $P(x, y)$ which divides the line segment joining $A(x_1, y_1)$ and $B(x_2, y_2)$ internally in the ratio $m_1 : m_2$ are $\left(\frac{m_1x_2 + m_2x_1}{m_1 + m_2}, \frac{m_1y_2 + m_2y_1}{m_1 + m_2}\right)$.

Proof Consider any two points $A(x_1, y_1)$ and $B(x_2, y_2)$ and assume that $C(x, y)$ divides AB, internally in the ratio $m_1 : m_2$,

i.e. $\frac{CA}{CB} = \frac{m_1}{m_2}$ [see Fig. 12.1]

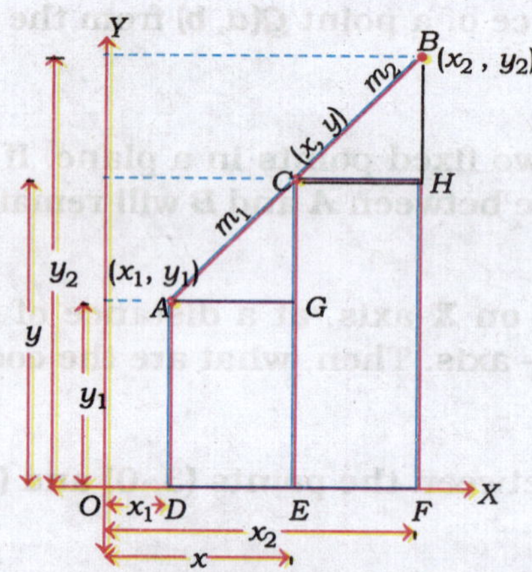

Fig. 12.1

Draw AD, CE and BF perpendicular to the X-axis. Draw AG and CH parallel to the X-axis.

Then, by the AA similarity criterion, $\Delta CAG \sim \Delta BCH$

Therefore, $$\frac{CA}{CB} = \frac{AG}{CH} = \frac{CG}{BH} \quad \ldots\text{(i)}$$

Also, we have,
$$AG = DE = OE - OD = x - x_1$$
$$CH = EF = OF - OE = x_2 - x$$
$$CG = CE - GE = CE - AD = y - y_1$$
$$BH = BF - HF = BF - CE = y_2 - y$$

On substituting these values in Eq. (i), we get $\dfrac{m_1}{m_2} = \dfrac{x - x_1}{x_2 - x} = \dfrac{y - y_1}{y_2 - y}$

$$\Rightarrow \quad \frac{m_1}{m_2} = \frac{x - x_1}{x_2 - x} \quad \text{and} \quad \frac{m_1}{m_2} = \frac{y - y_1}{y_2 - y}$$

$$\Rightarrow \quad x = \frac{m_1x_2 + m_2x_1}{m_1 + m_2} \quad \text{and} \quad y = \frac{m_1y_2 + m_2y_1}{m_1 + m_2}$$

So, the coordinates of the point $C(x, y)$ which divides the line segment, joining the points $A(x_1, y_1)$ and $B(x_2, y_2)$, internally in the ratio $m_1 : m_2$ are

$$\left(\frac{m_1x_2 + m_2x_1}{m_1 + m_2}, \frac{m_1y_2 + m_2y_1}{m_1 + m_2}\right)$$

This is known as **section formula.**

Procedure

1. Take a cardboard of suitable size and paste chart paper on it.
2. Also, paste a graph paper on the chart paper.
3. Draw the axes $X'OX$ and $Y'OY$ on the graph paper. (see Fig. 12.2)

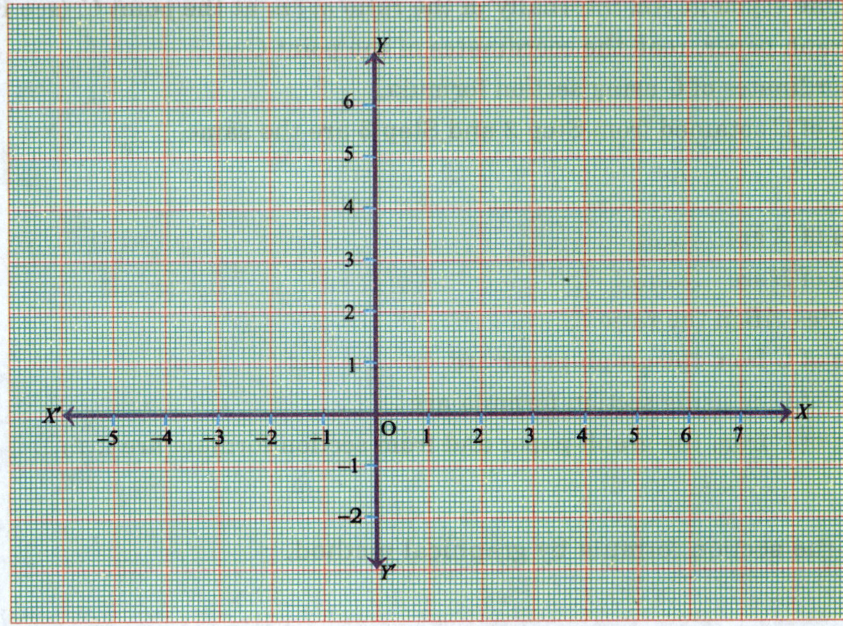

Fig. 12.2

4. Take two points, A having coordinates (x_1, y_1) and B having coordinates (x_2, y_2) on the graph paper. (see Fig. 12.3)
5. Join points A to B to get the line segment AB.
6. Draw CE parallel to BF with the help of ruler and compass.

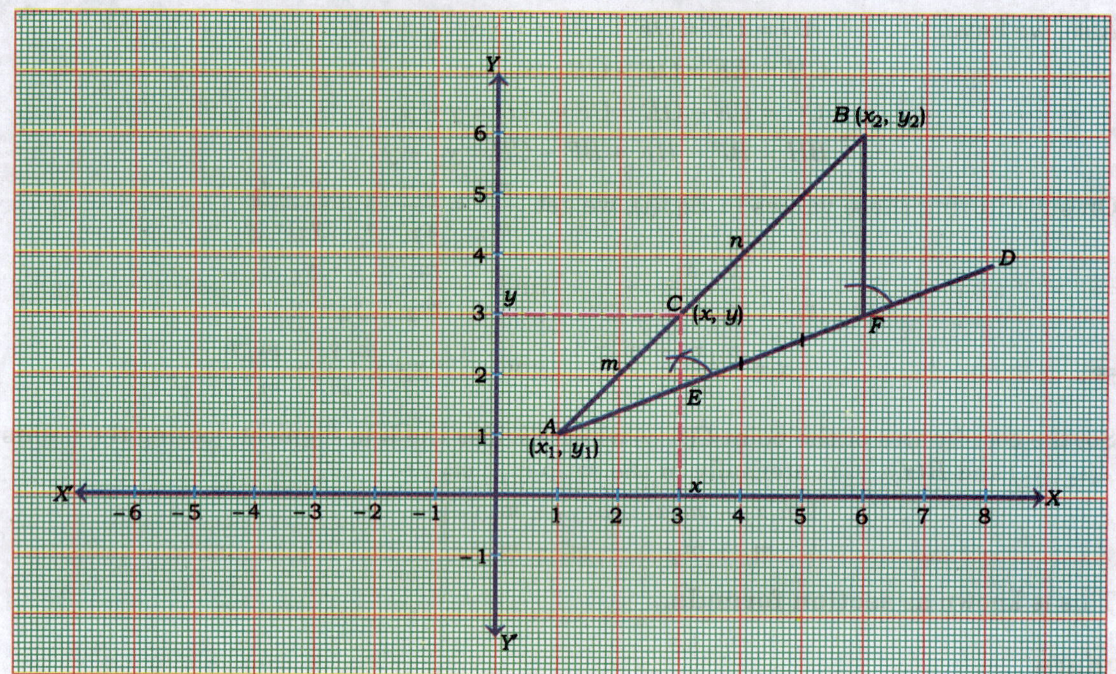

Fig. 12.3

Demonstration

1. Divide the line segment AB, internally in the ratio $m : n$, at the point C. (see Fig. 12.3)
2. From the graph paper, read the coordinates of the point C.
3. Find the coordinates of C using section formula.
4. Coordinates of C obtained from Step 2 and Step 3 are the same.

Observations

1. Coordinates of A are ....
2. Coordinates of B are ....
3. Point C divides AB in the ratio ....
4. Coordinates of C from the graph paper are......... .
5. Coordinates of C by using section formula are ....
6. Coordinates of C from the graph paper and from section formula are ....

Result

We have verified the section formula by graphical method.

Application

Centroid of a triangle in geometry, vector algebra and 3-dimensional geometry can be found using this formula.

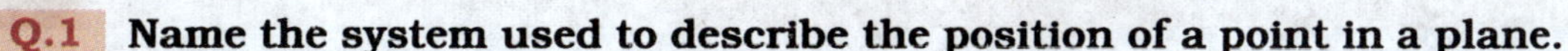

Viva-Voce

Q.1 Name the system used to describe the position of a point in a plane.

Ans Cartesian system

Q.2 The point where both x and y-coordinates are zero, is called ....

Ans. origin

Q.3 What is section formula?

Ans $\left(\frac{m_1x_2 + m_2x_1}{m_1 + m_2}, \frac{m_1y_2 + m_2y_1}{m_1 + m_2}\right)$

where, $m_1 : m_2$ is the ratio in which the line segment joining the points (x_1, y_1) and (x_2, y_2) is divided.

Q.4 What is mid-point formula for a line segment?

Ans $\left(\frac{x_1 + x_2}{2}, \frac{y_1 + y_2}{2}\right)$

where, (x_1, y_1) and (x_2, y_2) are ends points of the line segment.

Q.5 What is the condition to get mid-point of a line segment?

Ans If a point, divides the line segment, internally in ratio 1 : 1, then mid-point is obtained.

Q.6 What are trisection points?

Ans The points which divides the line segment into three equal segments, are called trisection points.

Activity 13

OBJECTIVE

To find the height of a building using a clinometer.

Prior Knowledge

1. Knowledge about clinometer (or sextant).
2. Trigonometric ratio (tan) for right angled triangle.
3. Understanding of the line of sight.
4. Understanding of the angle of elevation and depression.

Materials Required

1. Clinometer (a stand fitted with a square plate which is fitted with a movable 0° 360° protractor and a straw)
2. A measuring tape 50 m long
3. A table or stool

Theory

1. A clinometer is a fairly simple instrument which is used to measure the angle of a slope.
2. In a right angled triangle, trigonometric ratio $\tan\theta = \dfrac{\text{Perpendicular}}{\text{Base}}$

   where, side opposite to angle θ is perpendicular and side adjacent to it, is base.
3. The **line of sight** is the line drawn from the eye of an observer to the point in the object viewed by the observer.
4. **Angle of elevation** of an object is the angle formed by the line of sight with the horizontal, when it is above the horizontal level, i.e. the case when we raise our head to look at the object. (see Fig. 13.1)

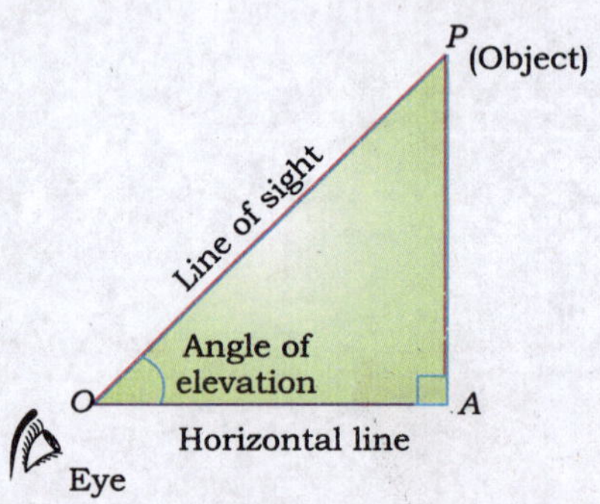

Fig. 13.1

5. **Angle of depression** of an object is the angle formed by the line of sight with the horizontal, when it is below the horizontal level, i.e. the case when we lower our on lead to look at the object. (see Fig. 13.2)

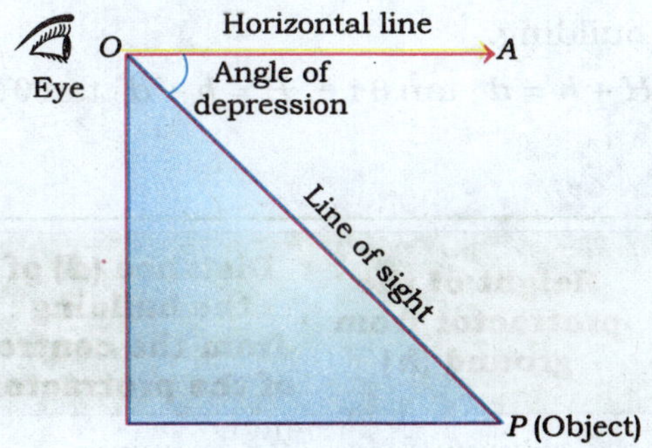

Fig. 13.2

Procedure

1. To measure the angle of elevation of the top of the school building, place a clinometer at a suitable location.
2. Peep out through the straw to the top of the school building and note the angle (θ) through which the protractor turns from 0° 360° line.
3. Measure the height (h) of the centre of the protractor from the ground.
4. Measure the distance (d) of the building from the point lying on the vertical line of the stand (centre of the protractor) kept on table. (see Fig. 13.3)
5. Repeat the above method keeping the clinometer at different positions and collect the values of θ, h, d for different settings.

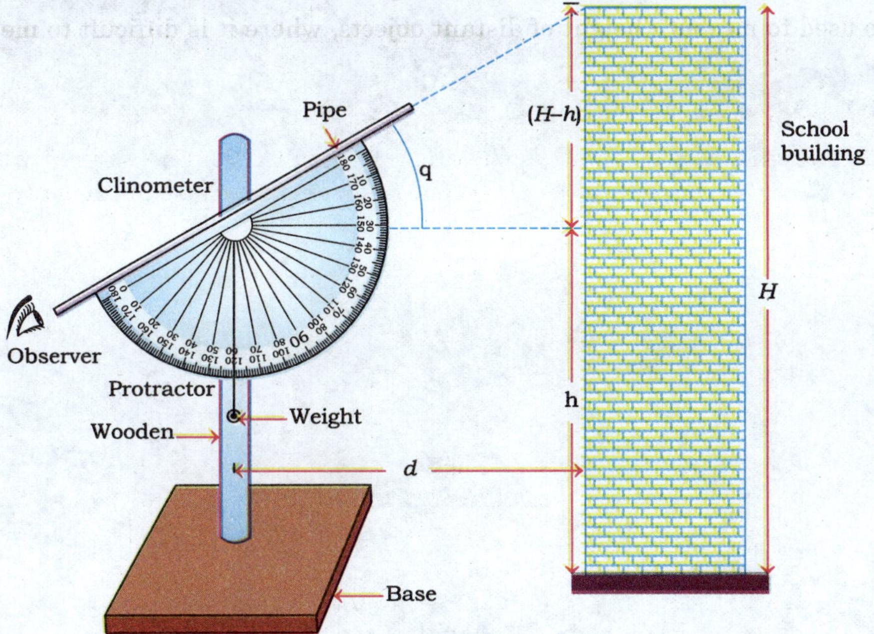

Fig. 13.3

Demonstration

Using the concept of trigonometric ratios, we have $\tan\theta = \frac{H-h}{d}$

where, H is the height of the building.

$\Rightarrow$ $H - h = d \cdot \tan\theta$ i.e. $H = h + d \cdot \tan\theta$

Observations

S.No.	Angle measured through protractor (angle of elevation) θ	Height of the protractor from ground (*h*)	Distance (*d*) of the building from the centre of the protractor	tan θ	Height of the building $H = h + d \tan\theta$
1.	....	....	....	....	....
2.	....	....	....	....	....
3.	....	....	....	....	....
4.	....	....	....	....	....
5.	....	....	....	....	....
6.	....	....	....	....	....
7.	....	....	....	....	....

Result

We have found the height of a building using clinometer.

Applications

1. A clinometer can be used in measuring an angle of elevation and an angle of depression.
2. It is also used to measure height of distant objects, where it is difficult to measure the height directly.

Viva-Voce

Q.1 What do you mean by clinometer?

Ans A clinometer is a geometrical instrument, in which a stand fitted with a square plate and a movable 0° to 360° protractor and a straw.

Q.2 How would you define the angle of elevation?

Ans Angle of elevation of an object is the angle formed by the line of sight with the horizontal, when it is above the horizontal level, i.e. the case when we raise our head to look at the object.

Q.3 How would you define the angle of depression?

Ans. Angle of depression of an object is the angle formed by the line of sight with the horizontal, when it is below the horizontal level, i.e. the case when we lower our head to look at the object.

Q.4 Does angle of elevation and angle of depression are always obtuse angles?

Ans No, the angles will be acute.

Q.5 How does angle of elevation get affected when height of tower, distance between the observer and foot of tower both are doubled?

Ans Angle of elevation remains same.

Q.6 When an observer moves towards the building, does angle of elevation increases or decreases?

Ans Increases

Q.7 If angle of elevation of the sun above a building decreases, then the length of shadow of a building......... .

Ans Increases

Q.8 What happens about the length of shadow of a tower, when the angle of elevation of sun above a tower decreases?

Ans The length of shadow of a tower will be increase.

Activity 14

OBJECTIVE

To verify experimentally that the tangent at any point to a circle is perpendicular to the radius through that point.

Prior Knowledge

1. Various terms related to a circle.
2. Tangent to a circle.

Materials Required

1. Coloured glazed papers
2. Adhesive
3. Scissors/Cutter
4. Geometry box
5. White chart paper

Theory

1. A circle is a collection of points which are at a fixed distance from a fixed point. The fixed point is called **centre** of the circle and fixed distance is called the **radius** of circle. (see fig. 14.1)

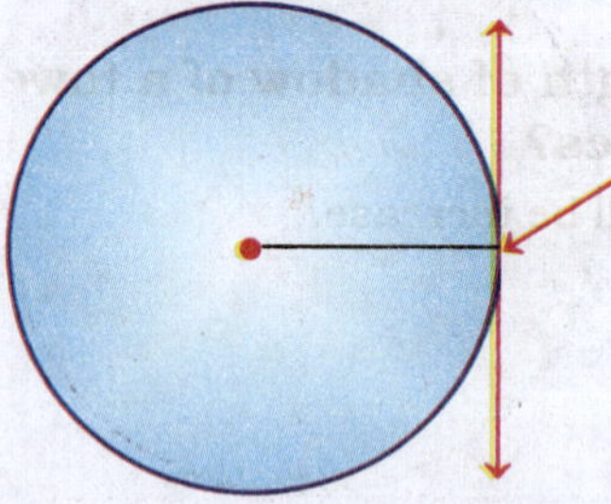

Fig. 14.1

2. If any line is drawn in such a way that it touches the circle at only one point, then such straight line is called **tangent** to the circle and the point at which it touches the circle is called **point of contact**. (see Fig. 14.1)

Procedure

1. Take a coloured glazed paper of suitable size and draw a circle of a suitable radius on it. Cut out this circle and paste it on a white chart paper.

2. Take any three points, A, B and C on the circle. (see Fig. 14.2)

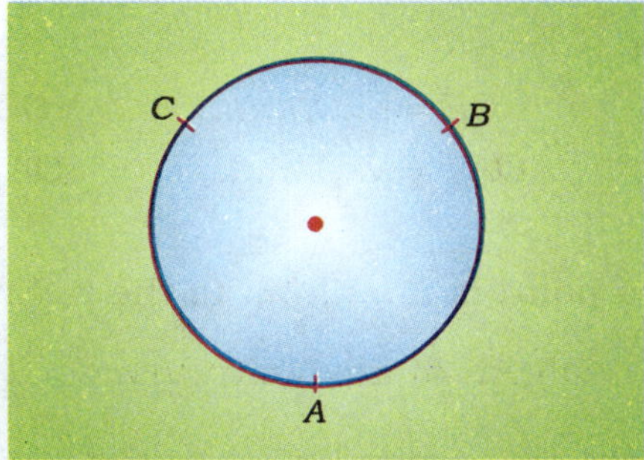

Fig. 14.2

3. Form a number of creases (by folding the paper through corners) through the three points, A, B and C. Out of these creases, select those which touch the circle. These creases will be tangents to the circle.
4. Let the creases intersect at the points P, Q and R, and forming a ΔPQR (see Fig. 14.3) (creases has been represented by dotted lines).
5. The circle now can be taken as incircle of ΔPQR with O as its centre. Join OA, OB and OC (see Fig. 14.3).
6. Take points A_1 and A_2 on the crease QR.

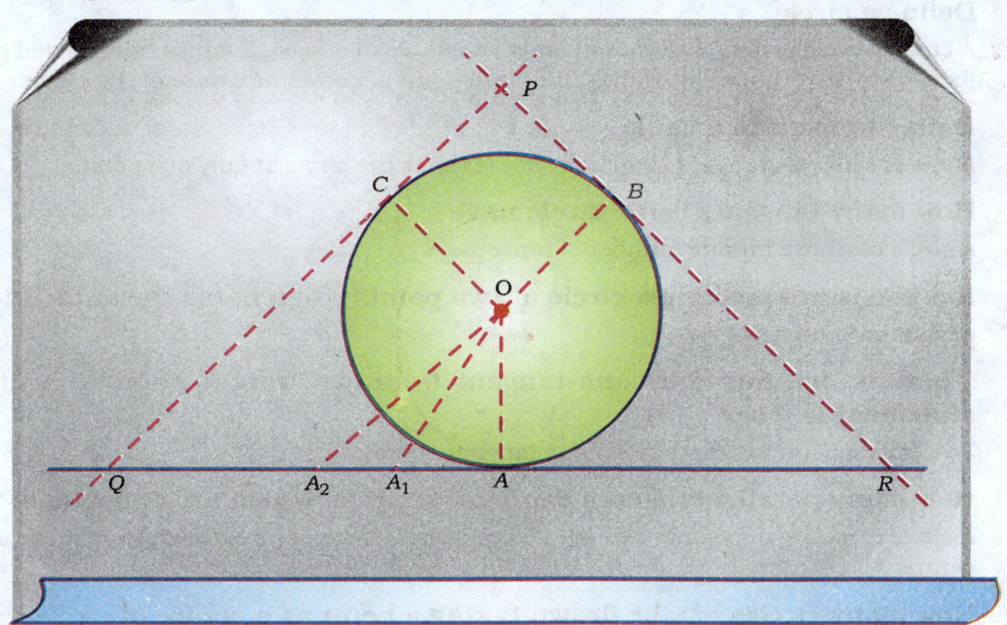

Fig. 14.3

Demonstration

Take triangles, ΔAOA_1 and ΔAOA_2.

Clearly, $OA_1 > OA$ and $OA_2 > OA$.

Also, OA is less than any other line segment, joining O to any point on QR other than A, i.e. OA is the shortest of all those.

Therefore, $OA \perp QR$. [$\because$ if a point on a line is at shortest distance from a fixed point, then the line joining these points is perpendicular to given line]

Hence, tangent to the circle at a point is perpendicular to the radius through that point. Similarly, it can be shown that $OB \perp PR$ and $OC \perp PQ$.

Observation

By actual measurement, we get

OA = ..., OB = ... , OC = ...,

OA_1 = ... , OA_2 = ..., $OA < OA_1$, OA .... OA_2

Therefore, OA .... QR

Hence, tangent to the circle at a point is .... to the radius through that point.

Result

The tangent at any point to a circle is perpendicular to the radius through that point has been verified experimentally.

Application

Various other results of geometry can be proved by using this result.

Viva-Voce

Q.1 Define a circle.

Ans A circle is a collection of all those points which are at a fixed distance from a fixed point, where fixed distance is known as radius and fixed point is known as centre of the circle.

Q.2 Define tangent to a circle.

Ans A line is said be a tangent to a circle, if it touches the circle at only one point.

Q.3 How many tangents can a circle have?

Ans A circle can have infinite number of tangents.

Q.4 If a line is intersecting a circle at two points, then name the such line.

Ans Secant (intersecting line)

Q.5 'There is one and only one tangent is drawn from a point to a circle'. Is this statement is true?

Ans Yes, from a point to a circle, only one tangent is drawn.

Q.6 How many parallel tangents can have a circle, which are opposite of the centre?

Ans A circle can have maximum two parallel tangents which can be drawn to opposite side of the centre.

Q.7 How many circles can be drawn taking a point as a centre of circle?

Ans Infinite circles can be drawn taking a point as a centre of circle.

Q.8 If a line which is perpendicular to the radius of the circle through the point of contact, then what will you call that line?

Ans Tangent

Q.9 The radius of two concentric circles are equal. (True/False)

Ans False

Q.10 The centre of two concentric circles are always same. (True/False)

Ans True

Activity 15

OBJECTIVE

To find the number of tangents from a point to a circle.

Prior Knowledge

1. Various terms related to a circle like radius, centre, etc.
2. Tangent to a circle.

Materials Required

1. Cardboard
2. Geometry box
3. Cutter
4. Different coloured sheets
5. Adhesive
6. Nails
7. String

Theory

1. For terms related to circle see Activity 14.
2. For tangent to a circle see Activity 14.

Procedure

1. Take a cardboard of suitable size and paste a coloured sheet on it.
2. Now, draw a circle of suitable radius on another coloured sheet and cut it out.
3. Paste the cut out, circle on the cardboard. (see Fig. 15.1)

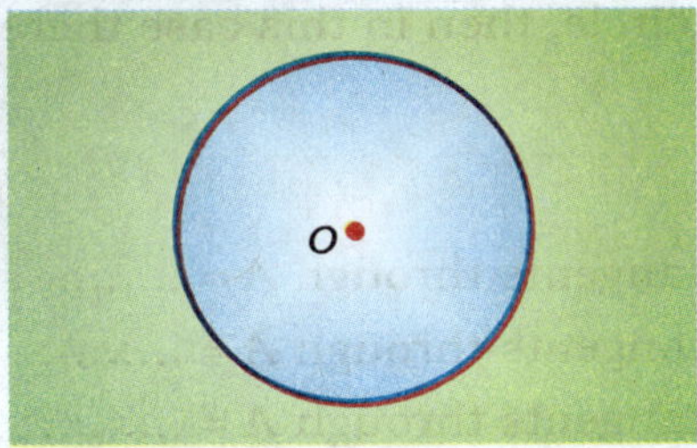

Fig. 15.1

4. Now, take any point A outside the circle or on the circle or inside the circle and fix a nail on it. (see Fig. 15.2, Fig. 15.3 and Fig. 15.4).

5. Take a string and tie one end of it at the point A and move the other end towards the centre of the circle. Also, move it up and down from the centre such that it may touch the circle. (see Fig. 15.2, Fig. 15.3 and Fig. 15.4)

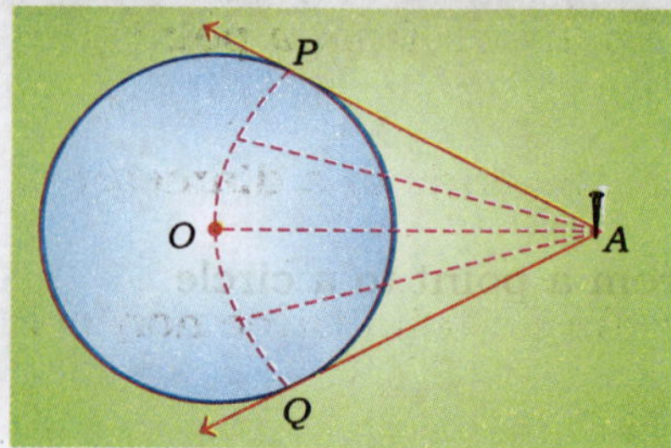

Fig. 15.2

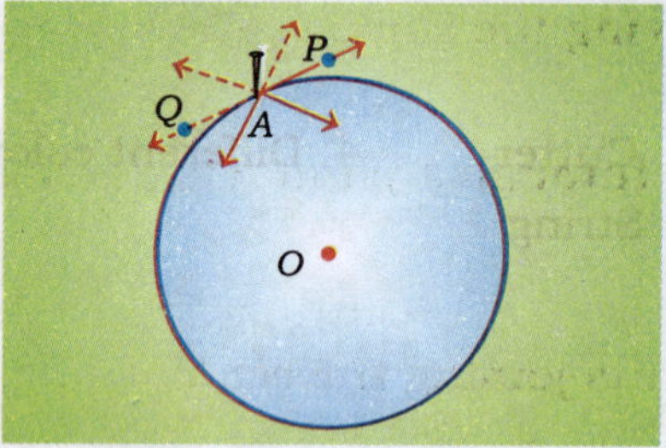

Fig. 15.3

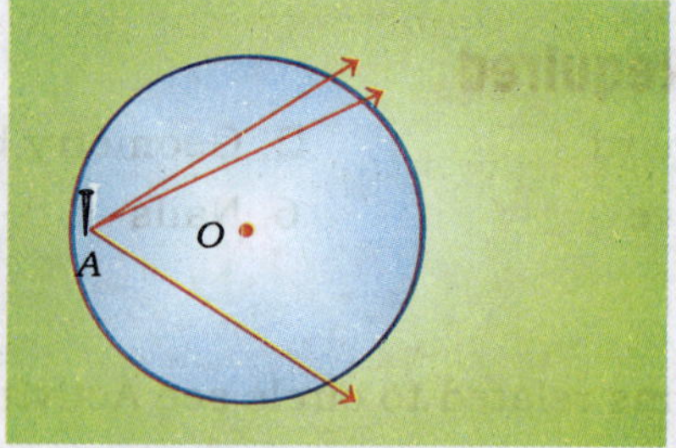

Fig. 15.4

Demonstration

1. If the point A lies outside the circle, then there are two tangents AP and AQ. (see Fig. 15.2)
2. If the point A is on the circle, then there is only one tangent at A. (see Fig. 15.3)
3. If the point A lies inside the circle, then in this case there is no tangent to the circle. (see Fig. 15.4)

Observations

1. In Fig. 15.2, the number of tangents through A = ...
2. In Fig. 15.3, the number of tangents through A = ...
3. In Fig. 15.4, the number of tangents through A = ...

Result

Number of tangents from a point to a circle has been found.

Application

This activity is useful in verifying the property that the lengths of the two tangents drawn from an external point are equal.

Viva-Voce

Q.1 **How many tangents can be drawn from a point present on the circle?**
Ans One

Q.2 **Are the tangents drawn at the ends of a diameter of a circle are parallel?**
Ans Yes

Q.3 **How many circles can be drawn from three non-collinear points?**
Ans Only one circle can be drawn.

Q.4 **How many circles can you draw from a given point?**
Ans Infinitely many circles can be drawn from a given point.

Q.5 **What is the name of two or more circles having the same centre?**
Ans Concentric circles

Q.6 **Can you draw a tangent to a circle passing through a point lying inside the circle?**
Ans No

Q.7 **What is the angle between tangent and radius joining the centre to point *P*, if *P* lies on the circle?**
Ans 90°

Q.8 **How many tangents can be drawn from an external point to a circle?**
Ans Only two tangents can be drawn from an external point to a circle.

Q.10 **We can draw a tengent from a point lying inside the circle (True/False).**
Ans False

Activity 16

OBJECTIVE

To verify that the lengths of tangents to a circle from some external point are equal.

Prior Knowledge

1. Various terms related to a circle.
2. Concept of tangent to a circle.
3. Length of tangent.

Materials Required

1. Glazed papers of different colours
2. Geometry box
3. Scissors
4. Adhesive

Theory

1. For terms related to circle see Activity 14.
2. For tangent to a circle see Activity 14.
3. A tangent, from external point (say) P to a circle is a straight line which touches the circle at a point, say A. Then, the length PA is called **length of tangent**. (see Fig. 16.1)

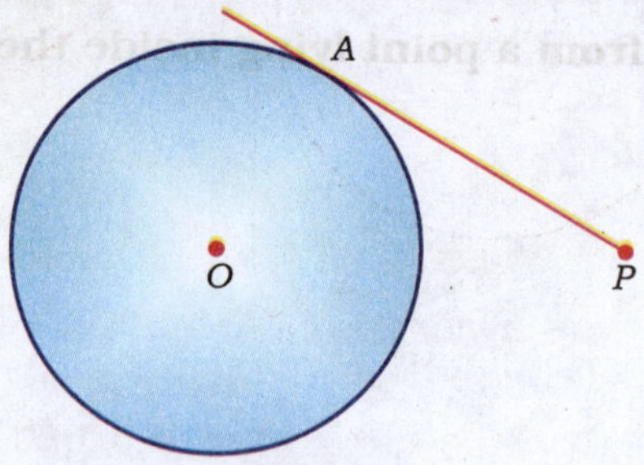

Fig. 16.1

Procedure

1. Take a coloured glazed paper of suitable size and draw a circle of any radius, say a units with centre O on it. (see Fig. 16.2)
2. Take any point P outside the circle. (see Fig. 16.2)

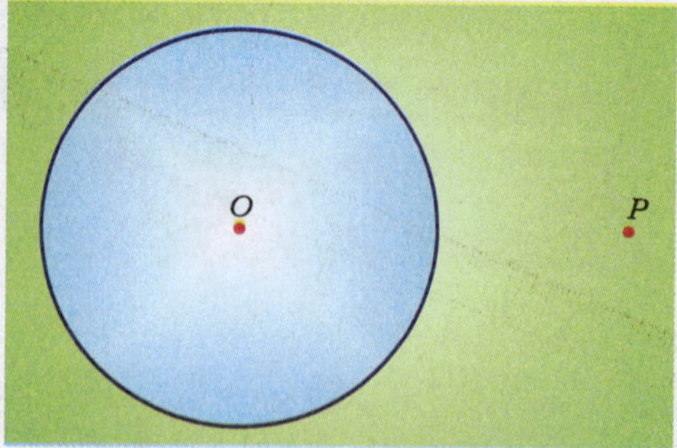

Fig. 16.2

3. Place a ruler touching the point P and the circle, lift the paper and fold it to create a crease in such a way that it passes through P and touches the circle. (see Fig. 16.3)

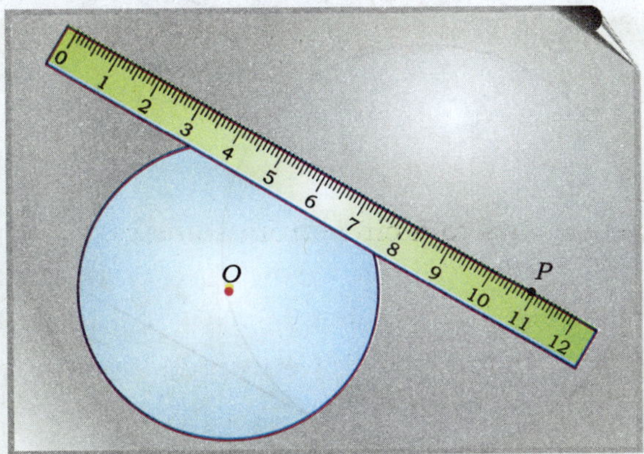

Fig. 16.3

4. The crease thus created is a tangent to the circle from the point P. Mark the point of contact of the tangent and the circle as A. Join PA. (see Fig. 16.4)

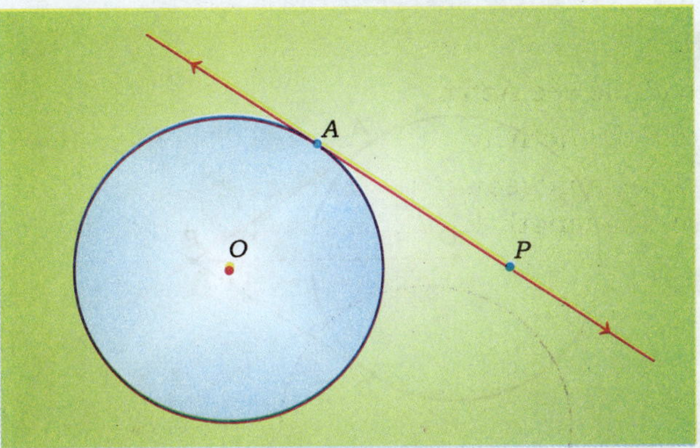

Fig. 16.4

5. Now, place ruler touching the point P and the other side of the circle, lift the paper and fold it to create a crease again in such a way that it passes through P and touches the circle. (see Fig. 16.5)

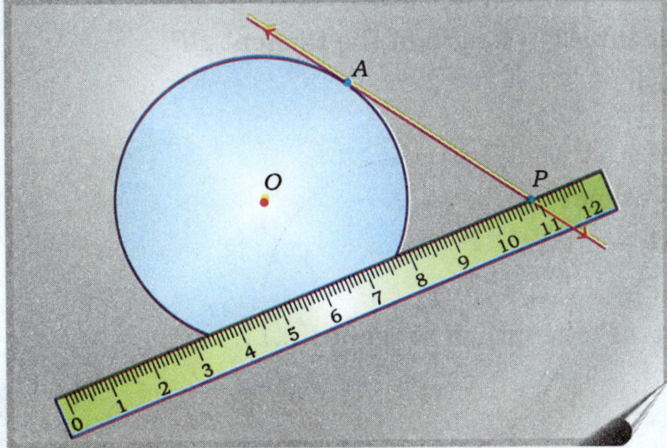

Fig. 16.5

6. This crease thus created is the second tangent to the circle from the point P. Mark the point of contact of the tangent and the circle as B. Join PB. (see Fig. 16.6)

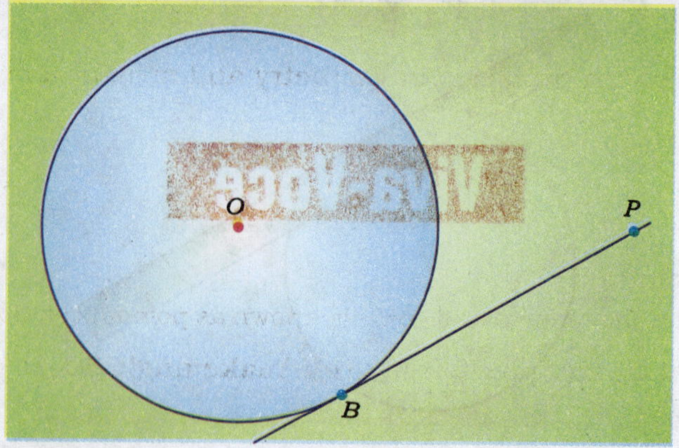

Fig. 16.6

7. Join centre of the circle O to the point P. (see Fig. 16.7)

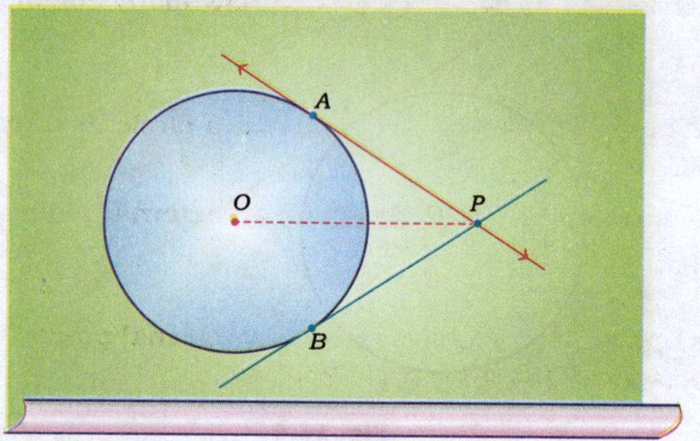

Fig. 16.7

Demonstration

1. Fold the circle along OP. (see Fig. 16.7)
2. We observe that A coincides with B. Therefore, $AP = BP$.

   i.e. length of the tangent AP = length of the tangent BP.

   This verifies the result.

Observations

On actual measurement, we get

1. Length of tangent AP = ...
2. Length of tangent BP = ...

   So, length of tangent AP = length of tangent ....

Result

We have verified that the lengths of tangents to a circle from same external point are equal.

Application

The activity is useful in solving problems in geometry and mensuration.

Viva-Voce

Q.1 Define point of contact.

Ans The common point of the tangent and circle is known as point of contact.

Q.2 Does the tangent at any point of a circle make angle 60° to the radius through the point of contact?

Ans No

Q.3 How many tangents can be drawn from an external point to a circle?

Ans Two

Q.4 If two circles intersect at two points, then how many common tangents can be drawn to the circles?

Ans Two

Q.5 Does a parallelogram drawn to circumscribe a circle, is a rectangle?

Ans No, it will be a square.

Q.6 Does two tangents drawn to a circle from an external point subtend unequal angles at the centre?

Ans No, they subtend equal angle.

Q.7 Two tangents are drawn to a circle from an external point, if the length of tangents are 3 cm and 4 cm. Does it happen?

Ans No, it cannot possible. The length of these tangents should be equal.

Q.8 Are the length of tangents to a circle from same external point equal or not?

Ans Yes, it is equal in lengths.

Activity 17

OBJECTIVE

To determine experimental probability of 1, 2, 3, 4, 5 or 6 by throwing a die 500 times and compare them with their theoretical probabilities.

Prior Knowledge

1. Outcomes of an experiment.
2. Favourable outcome.
3. Concept of probability.
4. Knowledge of a die.

Materials Required

1. A fair die
2. Pen
3. Sheets of white paper

Theory

1. An operation which can produce some well-defined outcomes is called an experiment. e.g. Tossing a coin is an experiment and in this experiment, we get either head or tail as a result, so head and tail are called **outcomes**.
2. The outcomes which ensure the occurrence of an event are called **favourable outcomes** to the event.
3. **Probability** If there are n outcomes associated with a random experiment and m of them are favourable to an event E, then the probability of happening or occurrence of event E is denoted by $P(E)$ and is defined as the ratio $\frac{m}{n}$.

Thus, probability of an event $E = P(E) = \frac{\text{Number of outcomes favourable to event } E}{\text{Total number of outcomes}}$

$$\Rightarrow \quad P(E) = \frac{m}{n}$$

Clearly, $0 \le m \le n$

$$\therefore \quad 0 \le \frac{m}{n} \le 1 \Rightarrow 0 \le P(E) \le 1$$

4. A die is a small cube having its six faces marked with dots (1 to 6).

A die

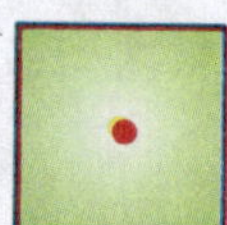
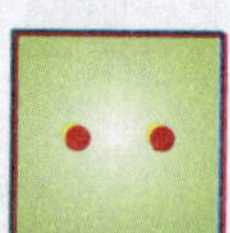
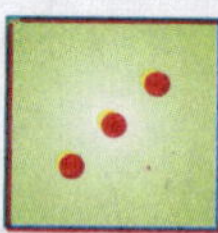
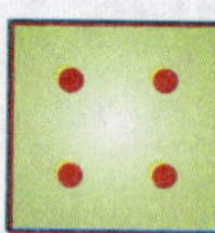
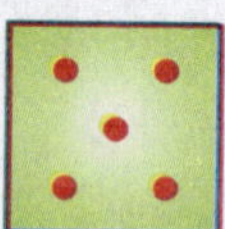
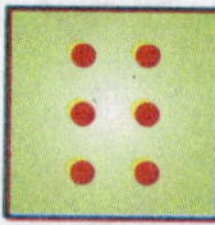

Six different faces of a die

Fig. 17.1

On throwing a die, any number from 1 to 6 can come, so total number of outcomes is 6. On throwing die, the chance of coming of any number from 1 to 6 is 1, so favourable outcome for any number from 1 to 6 will be 1.

$\therefore$ Probability of getting any number (from 1 to 6) on throwing a die

$$= \frac{\text{Number of favourable outcomes}}{\text{Total number of outcomes}} = \frac{1}{6}$$

Procedure

1. Divide the students of the class into ten groups I, II, III, IV, V, VI, VII, VIII, IX and X of suitable size.
2. Each group of students will throw a die 50 times and will observe the occurrence of each 1, 2, 3, 4, 5 and 6.
3. Count the total number of times (frequency) 1 comes up in each group and denote it by a_1, a_2, a_3, ..., a_{10}, respectively.
4. Calculate the experimental probability of 1 appearing each group as $\frac{a_1}{50}, \frac{a_2}{50}, \frac{a_3}{50}, \ldots, \frac{a_{10}}{50}$.
5. Calculate the experimental probability of 1 based on the data of 1st group, 1st two groups, ..., all the ten groups as
$$\frac{a_1}{50}, \frac{a_1 + a_2}{100}, \frac{a_1 + a_2 + a_3}{150}, \ldots, \frac{a_1 + a_2 + \ldots + a_{10}}{500}, \text{ respectively.}$$
6. Similarly, calculate the experimental probability of 2 based on the data of 1st group, 1st two groups, ..., all the ten groups as
$$\frac{b_1}{50}, \frac{b_1 + b_2}{100}, \frac{b_1 + b_1 + b_3}{150}, \ldots, \frac{b_1 + b_2 + \ldots + b_{10}}{500}, \text{ respectively.}$$
7. Proceed in the same way for getting experimental probabilities for 3, 4, 5 and 6.

Demonstration

1. The probability $\frac{a_1}{50}, \frac{a_1 + a_2}{100}, \frac{a_1 + a_2 + a_3}{150}, \ldots, \frac{a_1 + a_2 + \ldots + a_{10}}{500}$, are coming closer to $\frac{1}{6}$ and the last probability $\frac{a_1 + a_2 + \ldots + a_{10}}{500}$ is closest to $\frac{1}{6}$. Same will be the case for $\frac{b_1}{50}, \frac{b_1 + b_2}{100}, \frac{b_1 + b_2 + b_3}{150}, \ldots, \frac{b_1 + b_2 + \ldots + b_{10}}{500}$ and so on.
2. The theoretical probability $P(E)$ of an event E(say 1) = $P(1)$

$$\therefore \quad P(1) = \frac{\text{Number of outcomes favourable to } E}{\text{Number of all possible outcomes of the experiment}} = \frac{1}{6}$$

From steps (1) and (2), it can be seen that the experimental probability of each number 1, 2, 3, 4, 5 and 6 is very close to the theoretical probability $\frac{1}{6}$.

Group number	Number of times a die is thrown in a group	Total number of times a number comes up					
		1	2	3	4	5	6
I	50	a_1 =	b_1 =	c_1 =	d_1 =	e_1 =	f_1 =
II	50	a_2 =	b_2 =	-----	-----	-----	-----
III	50	-----	-----	-----	-----	-----	-----
—	—	-----	-----	-----	-----	-----	-----
—	—	-----	-----	-----	-----	-----	-----
—	—	-----	-----	-----	-----	-----	-----
—	—	-----	-----	-----	-----	-----	-----
—	—	-----	-----	-----	-----	-----	-----
—	—	-----	-----	-----	-----	-----	-----
X	50	-----	-----	-----	-----	-----	-----
	Total = 500	-----	-----	-----	-----	-----	-----

Observations

1. Each group will complete the following table

$\frac{a_1}{50} = \ldots\ldots,$ $\frac{a_1 + a_2}{100} = \frac{\sum_{i=1}^{2} a_i}{100} = \ldots\ldots,$ $\frac{\sum_{i=1}^{3} a_i}{150} = \ldots\ldots,$

$\frac{\sum_{i=1}^{4} a_i}{200} = \ldots\ldots,$ $\frac{\sum_{i=1}^{5} a_i}{250} = \ldots\ldots,$ $\frac{\sum_{i=1}^{6} a_i}{300} = \ldots\ldots,$

$\frac{\sum_{i=1}^{7} a_i}{350} = \ldots\ldots,$ $\frac{\sum_{i=1}^{8} a_i}{400} = \ldots\ldots,$ $\frac{\sum_{i=1}^{9} a_i}{450} = \ldots\ldots,$

$\frac{\sum_{i=1}^{10} a_i}{500} = \ldots\ldots.$

and same for b_i's, c_i's, ..., f_i's

2. Experimental probability of 1 = $\frac{\ldots.}{500}$

Experimental probability of 2 = $\frac{\ldots.}{500}$

....

....

Experimental probability of 6 = $\frac{\ldots.}{500}$

Experimental probability of 1 is nearly equal to theoretical ... .

Experimental probability of 2 is ...... to theoretical ....

Experimental probability of 6 is ...... to ...... probability.

Result

We have determined experimental probability of 1, 2, 3, 4, 5 and 6 by throwing a die 50 times and compared them with their theoretical probability, therefore the experimental probability of each number 1, 2, 3, 4, 5 and 6 is very closed to the theoretical probability $\frac{1}{6}$.

Application

Probability is used in the fields like physical science, commerce, biological science, medical science, weather forecasting, etc.

Viva-Voce

Q.1 What are favourable outcome(s) of an event?

Ans The outcome(s) which ensure(s) the occurrence of an event are called favourable outcome(s) to that event.

Q.2 How would you define the experimental or empirical probability of an event *E*?

Ans The experimental or empirical probability of an event *E* is

$$P(E) = \frac{\text{Number of trials in which the event occurred}}{\text{Total number of trials}}$$

Q.3 How would you define the theoretical probability (or classical probability) of an event *E*?

Ans The theoretical probability (or classical probability) of an event *E* is

$$P(E) = \frac{\text{Number of outcomes favourable to E}}{\text{Total number of possible outcomes of the experiment}}$$

Q.4 What do you mean by 'NEGATION' of an event?

Ans An event 'not *A*' occurs if and only if *A* does not occur. The event 'not A' is called negation of event *A* and is denoted by $\overline{A}$.

Q.5 What is the probability of a sure event?

Ans The probability of sure event is 1.

Q.6 What is the probability of an impossible event?

Ans The probability of an impossible event is 0.

Q.7 What is the relationship between the probability of an event *A* and the probability of negation of *A*?

Ans $P(A) + P(\overline{A}) = 1$

Q.8 If the probability of occurrence of an event is 0.4, then what is the probability that it does not occurs?

Ans $1 - 0.4 = 0.6$

Activity 18

OBJECTIVE

To determine experimental probability of a head (or a tail) by tossing a coin 1000 times and compare it with its theoretical probability.

Prior Knowledge

1. Outcomes of an experiment.
2. Favourable outcome.
3. Concept of probability.
4. Knowledge of a coin.

Materials Required

1. A fair coin
2. Pen
3. Sheets of white paper

Theory

1. For outcomes of an experiment see Activity 17.
2. For favourable outcomes see Activity 17.
3. For concept of probability see Activity 17.
4. A coin has two sides, head (*H*) and tail (*T*). (see Fig. 18.1)

Probability of getting a head or a tail on tossing a coin = $\frac{\text{Number of favourable outcomes}}{\text{Total number of outcomes}}$

Head

Tail

Fig. 18.1

On tossing a coin, there are two possible outcomes, i.e. head and tail, so total number of outcomes is 2. On tossing a coin, the chance of coming head or tail is 1, i.e. the number of favourable outcomes for head or tail is 1 because either head will come or tail.

∴ Probability of getting a head or a tail on tossing a coin = $\frac{1}{2}$

Procedure

1. Divide the students of the class into ten groups I, II, III, ..., X.
2. Now, each group will toss a coin 100 times and will observe the occurrence of a head.
3. Count the total number of times (frequency) a head comes up in each group and denote these by $a_1, a_2, ..., a_{10}$, respectively.
4. Calculate the experimental probability of a head in each group as $\frac{a_1}{100}, \frac{a_2}{100}, ..., \frac{a_{10}}{100}$.
5. Calculate the experimental probabilities of a head based on the data of 1st group, 1st two groups, ..., all ten groups as $\frac{a_1}{100}, \frac{a_1+a_2}{200}, \frac{a_1+a_2+a_3}{300}, ..., \frac{a_1+a_2+...+a_{10}}{1000}$, respectively.

Demonstration

1. The probabilities $\frac{a_1}{100}, \frac{a_1+a_2}{200}, \frac{a_1+a_2+a_3}{300}, ..., \frac{a_1+a_2+...+a_{10}}{1000}$, are coming closer and closer to $\frac{1}{2}$.
2. The theoretical probability of an event E (a head)

$$P(E) = \frac{\text{Number of outcomes favourable to } E}{\text{Number of all possible outcomes of the experiment}} = \frac{1}{2}$$

From points 1 and 2, it can be seen that the experimental probability of a head is very close to the theoretical probability.

This activity can be performed for the occurrence of a tail.

Observations

1. Each group will complete the following table

Group	Number of times a coin is thrown in a group	Total number of times a head comes up
I	100	a_1 = ...
II	100	a_2 = ...
III	100	a_3 = ...
IV	100	a_4 = ...
—	—	—
—	—	—
—	—	—
—	—	—
—	—	—
X	100	a_{10} = ...

2. $\frac{a_1}{100}$ = ..., $\frac{a_1+a_2}{200} = \frac{\sum_{i=1}^{2} a_i}{200}$ = ..., $\frac{\sum_{i=1}^{3} a_i}{300}$ = ... ,

$\frac{\sum_{i=1}^{4} a_i}{400}$ = ..., $\frac{\sum_{i=1}^{5} a_i}{500}$ =......, $\frac{\sum_{i=1}^{6} a_i}{600}$ = ...,

$$\frac{\sum_{i=1}^{7} a_i}{700} = \ldots\ldots, \quad \frac{\sum_{i=1}^{8} a_i}{800} = \ldots\ldots, \quad \frac{\sum_{i=1}^{9} a_i}{900} = \ldots\ldots, \quad \frac{\sum_{i=1}^{10} a_i}{1000} = \ldots\ldots$$

3. Experimental probability of a head = $\frac{\ldots\ldots}{1000}$
4. Experimental probability of a head is nearly equal to theoretical ... .
5. ...... probability of a head is nearly ...... to theoretical ....

Result

We have determined experimental probability of a head (or a tail) by tossing a coin 100 times and compared it with its theoretical probability. Thus, experimental probability of a head is nearly equal to theoretical probability.

Application

Probability is used extensively in the fields like physical sciences, commerce, biological sciences, medical sciences, weather forecasting, etc.

Viva-Voce

Q.1 What do you mean by an event?

Ans An event for an experiment is the collection of some outcomes of the experiment.

Q.2 Define equally likely outcomes.

Ans The outcomes of a random experiment are said to be equally likely, when each outcome is as likely to occur as the other, i.e. when we have no reason to believe that one is more likely to occur than the other.

Q.3 What is a compound event?

Ans An event associated to a random experiment is a compound event, if it is obtained by combining two or more elementary events associated to the random experiment.

Q.4 What is the sum of the probabilities of all the outcomes (elementary events) of an experiment?

Ans One

Q.5 Name some areas in which probability has been used in recent years.

Ans The areas in which probability has been commonly used, are Mathematics, Biology, Economics, Genetics, Physics, Sociology, etc.

Q.6 What are the possible outcomes if a coin is tossed twice?

Ans HH, HT, TH, TT.

Q.7 If a die is thrown, then what is the probability that an odd number will come?

Ans $\frac{3}{6} = \frac{1}{2}$.

Project 1

OBJECTIVE

Chronological development of solution of a quadratic equations.

Solution of a Quadratic Equations

1. Euclid

Euclid, the Greek mathematician, produced a more abstract geometrical method about 300 BC with purely geometric approach, Pythagoras and Euclid created a general procedure to find the solutions of the quadratic equation.

In his work Arithmetica, *the Greek mathematician Diophantus solved the quadratic equation but gave only one root, even when both roots were positive.*

2. Babylonians

Babylonian mathematician as early as 2000 BC could solve problems relating the areas and sides of rectangles. In modern notation, the problems typically involved in solving a pair of simultaneous equations of the form

$$x + y = p \ ; \ xy = q$$

which are equivalent to the equation

$$x^2 + q = px.$$

The steps given by Babylonian scribes for solving the above rectangular problem as follows:

(i) Compute half of p.

(ii) Square the result.

(iii) Subtract q from it.

(iv) Find the square root using a table of squares.

(v) Add together the results obtained in Step (i) and Step (iv).

This is essentially equivalent to calculating

$$x = \frac{p}{2} + \sqrt{\left(\frac{p}{2}\right)^2 - q}$$

Geometrical methods were used to solve the quadratic equations in Babylonia, Egypt, Greece, China and India.

In 8th century BC, quadratic equations of the form $ax^2 = c$ and $ax^2 + bx = c$ were explored using the geometric methods.

Babylonian mathematician from 400 BC *and Chinese mathematician from* 200 BC *used geometric method of dissection to solve the quadratic equations with positive roots.*

3. Brahmagupta

In 628 AD, Brahmagupta, an Indian mathematician gave the first explicit solution of the quadratic equation $ax^2 + bx = c$ as follows:

(i) To the absolute number multiplied by four times to the product of a and c, then add it with the square of the middle term (b).

(ii) In the second step, take the square root of the result obtained in Step (i), then less the middle term (b) from it.

(iii) In the last step, divide the result obtained in Step (ii) by the twice of a, which gives the result

$$x = \frac{\sqrt{4ac + b^2} - b}{2a}$$

4. Bakhshali Manscript

The Bakhshali Manscript written in India in the 7th century AD, contained an algebraic formula for solving quadratic equation as well as quadratic indeterminate equations.

5. Al-Khwarizmi

Al-Khwarizmi, an Islamic mathematician of 9th century, inspired by Brahmagupta and developed a set of formulae that worked for positive solutions. He goes further in providing a full solution to the general quadratic equation and accepting one or two numerical answers for every quadratic equations, while providing geometric proofs in the process.

He also described the method of completing the square and recognised that the discriminant must be positive, which was proven by his contemporary Abd-al-Hamid-ibn-Turk, who gave the geometric figure to prove that if the discriminant is negative, a quadratic equation has no solution. While Al-Khwarizmi himself did not accept negative solutions.

Later, Islamic mathematician succeeded to accepted negative as well as irrational numbers as solutions.

Project 2

OBJECTIVE

Sum of the exterior angles of a polygon taken in an order.

Prior Knowledge

1. Knowledge of regular or irregular polygon.
2. Knowledge of exterior angles to given angles.
3. Knowledge of results based on interior angles of a polygon.

Theory

1. A simple closed curve made up of only the line segments is called a **polygon**. If all the line segments are equal, then it is called regular polygon and if all the line segments are not equal, then it is called **irregular polygon**.
2. The **exterior angle** is formed by extending the side of the polygon.
3. The sum of the interior angles of a polygon having n sides is $180°(n -$

Description

Let $a_1, a_2, a_3, a_4, a_5, a_6, ..., a_n$ be the interior angles of n sided polygon.

Clearly, Exterior angle = 180° – Interior angle

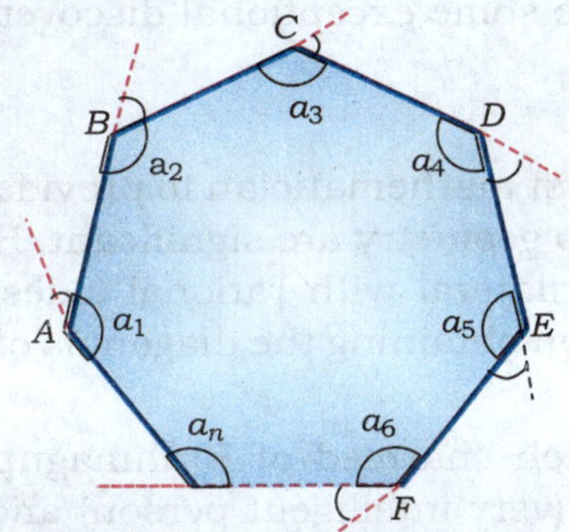

$\therefore$ The sum of all exterior angles of a polygon,

$$S = \text{exterior } \angle A + \text{exterior } \angle B + \text{exterior } \angle C + ...$$
$$= (180° - a_1) + (180° - a_2) + (180° - a_3) + ... + (180° - a_n)$$
$$= 180° + 180° + ... + \text{upto } n - (a_1 + a_2 + a_3 + ... + a_n)$$
$$= n(180°) - [180°(n-2)] = n(180°) - n(180°) + 360° = 360°$$

Learning Outcome

We learnt that the sum of the exterior angles of a polygon (triangle, quadrilateral, pentagon, etc.) taken in an order is 360°.

Project 3

OBJECTIVE

Indian Mathematicians and their contributions.

Materials Required

Fevistick, photographs of some famous Indian Mathematicians and a pair of scissors.

Aryabhata (476-550 AD)

Aryabhata wrote the first mathematics book in the world, called the Aryabhatiya. He also made significant contributions to astronomy, including calculating the value of pi.

Aryabhata's most significant contribution to mathematics was his development of algebraic methods. Algebra is a branch of mathematics that deals with manipulating equations and expressions. He developed the concept of zero by realising that the number zero can be used to represent the absence of a number. He also showed that zero could be used as a placeholder in mathematical equations.

Srinivasa Ramanujan (1887-1920 AD)

One of the greatest mathematicians of all time, Srinivasa Ramanujan was born in 1887 in the Southern part of India. He is still remembered for his contributions to the field of mathematics. Theorems formulated by him are to date studied by students across the world and within very few years of his lifespan, he made some exceptional discoveries in mathematics.

Brahmagupta (598-668 AD)

Brahmagupta (AD 628) was the first mathematician to provide the formula for the area of a cyclic quadrilateral. His contributions to geometry are significant. He is the first person to discuss the method of finding a cyclic quadrilateral with rational sides. His celebrated theorems on the circumdiameter of a triangle and on obtaining the diagonals of a cyclic quadrilateral are now well known.

Bhaskara II (AD 1150) is so much charmed of Brahmagupta's intellect that he respectfully refers to him as "Mahamatiman" (very intelligent person) and even confers the unique "Ganita Chakra Chudamani" (the gem of the circle of mathematicians) title on Brahmagupta.

Jaynata Vishnu Narlikar

Jaynata Vishnu Narlikar whom the world hailed as the Einstein of India.

He is the Mathematician turned Astrophysicist, internationally famous for his work on cosmetology. He championed the 'Steady state' theory alternative to the popular big bang theory of universe when he was only 26.

Born on July 19,1938 in Kolhapur, Maharashtra, Narlikar received his early education in the campus of Banaras Hindu University. After a brilliant career in school and college, he went to Cambridge for higher studies in Mathematics. He got his cambridge degree in Mathematics. He got specialization in Astronomy and Astrophysics.

His Contributions in Mathematics are linked below

1. The theory of the 'Steady state' universe.
2. **Hoyle-Narlikar Theory** A new theory of gravitation, which was then considered as significant as Einstein's theory of relativity.
3. White hole concept as exploding source of energy.
4. Pioneering experiment designed to sample air for microorganism in the atmoshpere at height of upto 41 km, which opened the intriguing possibility that earth is being bombarded by microorganism, some of which might have seeded life itself on earth.
5. Pioneering research on Astrophysics and Astronomy, in India.

Honours

Praises titles and rewards that JV Narlikar received, in India and in other countries are innumerable. Few of them are given below:

1. Padma Bushan 1965.
2. Padma Vibhushan 2004.
3. Indira Gandhi Award of National Science Academy 1990.
4. Kalinga Award by the UNESCO 1996.
5. Several National and International Award and Honorary Dectorates.
6. Shanti Swarup Bhatnagar Award.
7. MP Birla Award.

Project 4

OBJECTIVE

List some quotations of famous Mathematicians.

List of Quotations of Famous Mathematicians

1. Do not worry about your difficulties in Mathematics. I can assure you mine are still greater.

Albert Einstein

2. Mathematics is not about numbers, equations, computations or algorithms, it is about UNDERSTANDING.

William Paul Thurston

3. *A mathematical theory is not to be considered complete until you have made it so clear that you can explain it to the first man whom you meet on the street.*

David Hilbert

4. Without Mathematics, there's nothing you can do. Everything around you, is Mathematics. Everything around you, is numbers.

Shakuntala Devi

5. Mathematics, is, I believe, the chief source of the belief in eternal and exact truth, as well as a sensible intelligible world.

Bertrand Russell

6. Each problem that I solved became a rule which served afterwards to solve other problems.

Rene Descartes

7. Mathematics, even in its present and most abstract state, is not detached from life. It is just the ideal handling of the problems of life.

Cassius Jackson Keyser

8. Mathematics is pure language i.e. the language of science. It is unique among languages in its ability to provide precise expression for every thought or concept that can be formulated in its terms.

A. Adler

9. Equations are just the boring part of Mathematics. I attempt to see things in terms of geometry.

Stephen Hawking

Project 5

OBJECTIVE

Ramanujan Number (1729)

Theory

Srinivasa Ramanujan (22nd December 1887-26 April 1920) was renowned Indian mathematician. Inspite of having no formal training in pure Mathematics, Ramanujan made substantial contributions in the areas of mathematical analysis, number theory, infinite series and continued fractions. He independently complied nearly 3500 results during his short life time.

1729 came to be known as Ramanujan's number, after an interesting incident that took place between Ramanujan and his mentor, GH Hardy.

Once, Hardy was paying a visit to Ramanujan, who was ill and undergoing treatment at Putney (London). Hardy mentioned to him that he rode a taxi-cab, whose number was 1729. "The number 1729 seemed to me rather a dull one", he added.

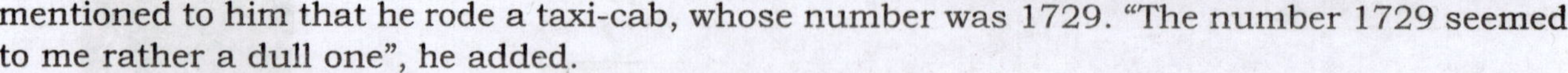

It is said about Ramanujan that the numbers 1-10000 were his **personal friends**. He could effortlessly tell you their factors, divisors, how the number can be split and the each part of the number can be squared/cubed, etc., to produce interesting numbers and much more.

Interestingly enough, Ramanujan replied to Hardy's comment, saying that 1729 is not a dull number at all. It is the smallest number that can be written as the sum of two cubes in two different ways.

This is meant by Ramanujan

$$\boxed{1729 = 12^3 + 1^3 = 10^3 + 9^3}$$

After Hardy told this incident to his colleagues, this number became well known and was called as Ramanujan's number.

Later on, numbers having similar property were also called Ramanujan's number and the problem of finding such numbers came to be known as Taxi-cab (2) problem.

Other example of such problem is 4104, which can be written as $4104 = (16^3 + 2^3)$ or $(15^3 + 9^3)$.

Project 6

OBJECTIVE

Mathematical Crosswords

Prior Knowledge

We must be familiar with crossword.

Theory

Definition of Crossword

A puzzle consisting of a grid of squares and blanks into which words crossing vertically and horizontally are written according to clues i.e. hints.

Procedure

Read the given clues related to mathematical crossword carefully and then fill the crossword.

Example 1. Clues of the following crossword are given as

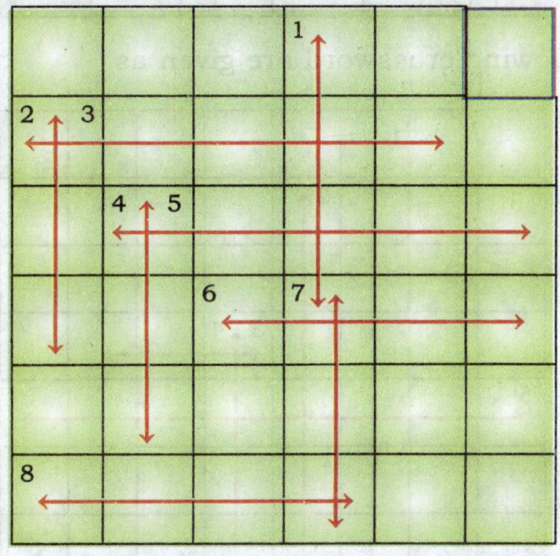

Across (Horizontally)

3. It is the solution of $8 - 2(x + 1) = 4x - 3(x + 5)$.
5. It is the solution of $2(x + 1)(x + 3) + 8 = (2x + 1)(x + 5)$.
6. If $3x - y = 15$, it is the value of x when y equals minus three.
8. It is the solution of $7(x - 2) = 3x + 22$.

Down (Vertically)

1. It is the value of x for the equation $\dfrac{5}{x-10} = \dfrac{6}{x-12}$, $x \neq 10, 12$.
2. This is the value of k, if $y = 9$ is a solution of the equation $y = \dfrac{3}{2}k$.
4. It is a solution of $\dfrac{3x-1}{4} + \dfrac{3}{4} = 2$.
7. It is the value of x, if $54 : 6x = 9 : 1$

Answer

			1 Z		
2 3 S	E	V	E	N	
I	4 5 T	H	R	E	E
X	W	6 F	7 O	U	R
	O		N		
8 N	I	N	E		

Example 2. Clues of the following crossword are given as

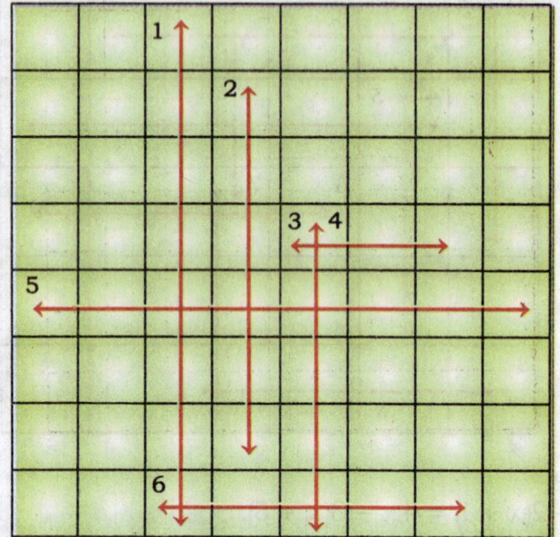

Across (Horizontally)

4. Data in its orginal form is called......data.
5. A quantity that takes different values in different situations.
6. An outcome associated with same experiment.

Down (Vertically)

1. These variables can take only integral values.
2. This is the middle most observation of a distribution.
3. This is the difference between the maximum and minimum values of the variate.

Answer

		1 D					
		I	2 M				
		S	E				
		C	D	3 4 R	A	W	
5 V	A	R	I	A	B	L	E
		E	A	N			
		T	N	G			
		6 E	V	E	N	T	

Do yourself

(i) Clues of the following mathematical crossword are given as

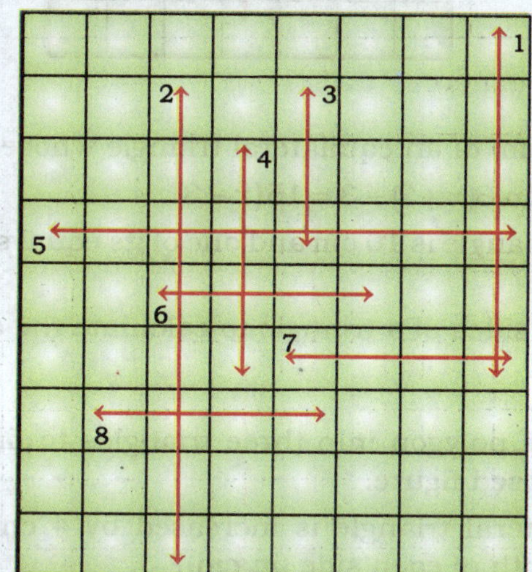

Across (Horizontally)

5. These numbers can be expressed in the form of $\frac{p}{q}$, where p, q are integers and $q \neq 0$.

6. These numbers are multiples of 2.

7. This is the value of x, if $2^{x-2} = 128$.

8. If $\frac{7+\sqrt{5}}{7-\sqrt{5}} + \frac{7-\sqrt{5}}{7+\sqrt{5}} = p + 7\sqrt{5}q$, then this is the value of q.

Down (Vertically)

1. If $x = 6 - \sqrt{35}$, then this is the value of $x + \frac{1}{x}$.
2. 7 and – 3 are the examples of this type of numbers.
3. If $\frac{\sqrt{2}+\sqrt{3}}{3\sqrt{2}-2\sqrt{3}} = a + b\sqrt{6}$, then this is the value of a.
4. This is the value of the expression $\frac{1}{\sqrt{9}-\sqrt{8}} - \frac{1}{\sqrt{8}-\sqrt{7}} + \frac{1}{\sqrt{7}-\sqrt{6}} - \frac{1}{\sqrt{6}-\sqrt{5}} + \frac{1}{\sqrt{5}-\sqrt{4}}$.

(ii) Clues of the following mathematical crossword are given as

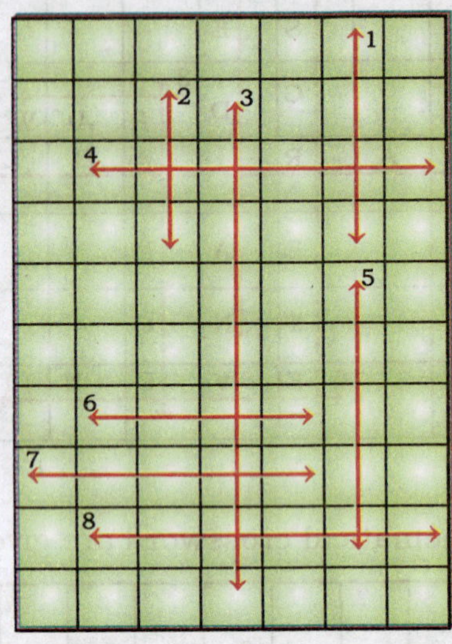

Across (Horizontally)

4. This is the perimeter (in cm) of an equilateral triangle whose altitude is $2\sqrt{3}$ cm.
6. The value of the expression $3(x + 2) - 3 = 15(x - 3)$
7. The base of an isosceles triangle is 10 cm and one of its equal sides is 13 cm. This is the area of given triangle (in cm^2).
8. This formula uses all the sides of a triangle to calculate the area of a triangle.

Down (Vertically)

1. A student divides a plane polygon into three triangles to find its area. Then, this is the number of sides of the closed figure.
2. If each side of an equilateral triangle is increased by 4 cm, then its area increases by $6\sqrt{3}$ cm^2, what is the length of each side (in cm)?
3. This is another name (unit) for 100 m.
5. If area of an isosceles right angled triangle is 24.5 cm^2, then this is the length of each of its equal sides (in cm).

Project 7

OBJECTIVE

Application of Geometry in day-to-day life.

Prior Knowledge

We must be familiar with similar triangles and basic theorems.

Mateiral Required

Geometry box and measuring tape.

Theory

Two triangles are said to be similar, if

(i) their corresponding angles are equal.

(ii) their corresponding sides are proportional i.e. the ratios of the lengths of corresponding sides are same.

Procedure

1. Let us find the height of a tower.
2. Observe the direction of shadow of the a tower.
3. Place the ruler vertically in the shadow of the tower so that the ends of its shadow is at the same place as the ends of the shadow of the tower.
4. Now, measure the distance of shadow of the tower, height of ruler and distance of the ruler from the tip of the ruler's shadow. Then, calculate the height of the tower by using the result of similar triangles.

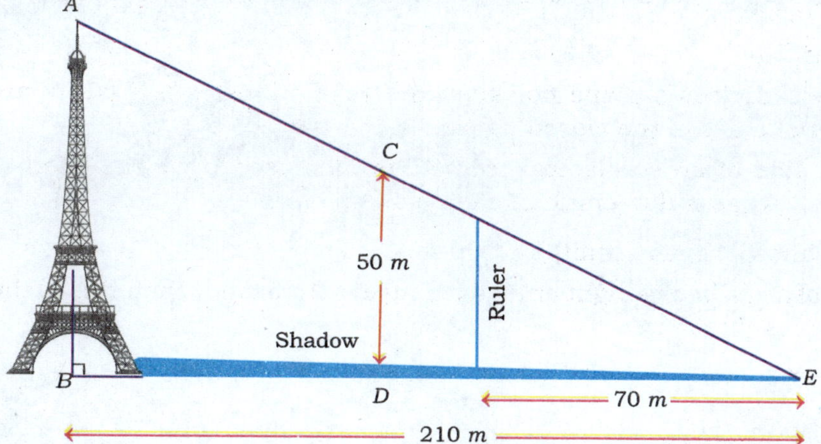

Example

Let AB and CD be the heights of tower and ruler, respectively and BE and DE be the distances of shadows of tower and ruler, respectively.

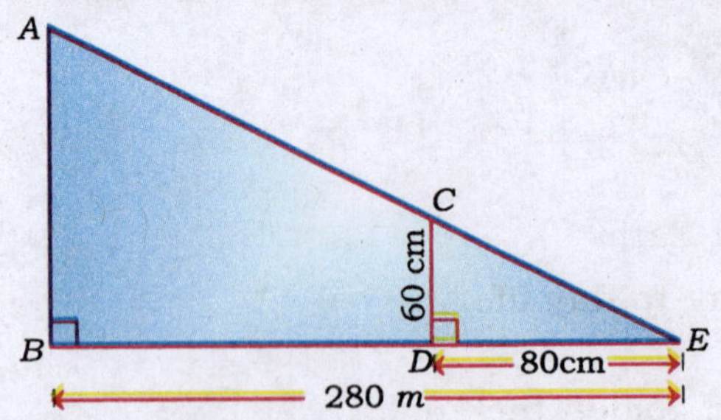

On measuring the length of shadows with measuring tape, we have

$BE = 280 \text{ m} = 28000 \text{ cm}$ [$\because 1 \text{ m} = 100 \text{ cm}$]

and $DE = 80 \text{ cm}$

On measuring CD (height of ruler), we get

$CD = 60 \text{ cm}$

We know that two right angled triangles with same base are always similar.

$\therefore \quad \Delta ABE \sim \Delta CDE$ [by AA similarity]

$\frac{AB}{CD} = \frac{BE}{DE}$ [by CPCT]

$\Rightarrow \quad AB = \frac{BE \times CD}{DE}$

$\Rightarrow \quad AB = \frac{\ldots \times \ldots}{\ldots}$

$\Rightarrow \quad AB = \ldots \text{ cm}$

$\Rightarrow \quad AB = \ldots \text{ m}$

Hence, the required height of the tower = ... m.

Project 8

OBJECTIVE

Golden Rectangle and Golden Ratio.

Prior Knowledge

Knowledge of golden ratio and golden rectangle.

Theory

1. **Golden ratio** is a special number, found by dividing a line into two parts so that the longer part divided by smaller part is also equal to the whole length divided by the longer part.
2. In geometry, a **golden rectangle** is a rectangle, the lengths of whose sides are in the golden ratio.

   In other words, a rectangle is said to be a golden rectangle, if it can be divided into two parts such that one part is a square and other part is a rectangle similar to the original rectangle.

Concept of Golden Ratio and Golden Rectangle

1. In the following figure, rectangle *ABCD* has been divided into a square *APQD* and a rectangle *QPBC*.

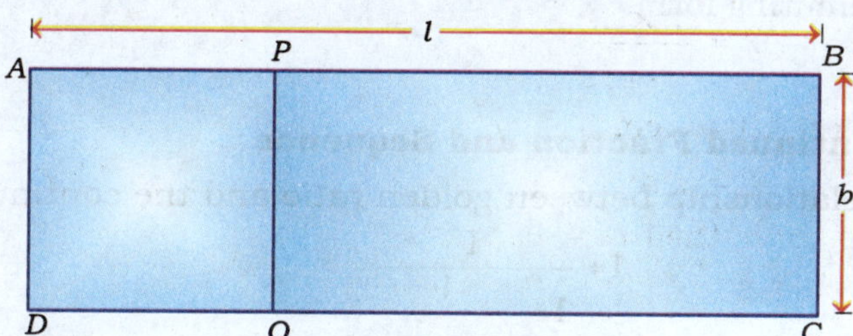

If the rectangle *QPBC* is similar to rectangle *ABCD*, then we can say that *ABCD* is a golden rectangle. Let $AB = l$ and $BC = b$. Therefore , $QP = b$.

Now, as $ABCD \sim QPBC$, we have

$$\frac{AB}{BC} = \frac{QP}{PB}$$

or $\quad \frac{l}{b} = \frac{b}{l-b} \quad$ or $\quad l^2 - lb = b^2$

or $\quad l^2 - lb - b^2 = 0 \quad$ or $\quad \left(\frac{l}{b}\right)^2 - \frac{l}{b} - 1 = 0 \quad$ ...(i)

Let $\frac{l}{b} = x$. So, from Eq. (i), we have

$$x^2 - x - 1 = 0$$

or $\quad x = \frac{1 \pm \sqrt{(-1)^2 - 4 \times (1)(-1)}}{2 \times 1} = \frac{1 \pm \sqrt{5}}{2} \quad$ [solving the quadratic equation]

Now, as x cannot be negative, therefore $x = \frac{\sqrt{5}+1}{2}$

Thus, $\frac{l}{b} = \frac{\sqrt{5}+1}{2}$

i.e. for a rectangle to become a golden rectangle, the ratio of its length and breadth $\left(\frac{l}{b}\right)$ must be $\frac{\sqrt{5}+1}{2}$. This ratio $\frac{\sqrt{5}+1}{2}$ is called the golden ratio. Its value is about 1.618.

Thus, it can be seen that the golden ratio is the ratio of the sides of a golden rectangle.

2. **Golden Ratio and Continued Fraction** Let us consider a continued fraction

$$1+\cfrac{1}{1+\cfrac{1}{1+\ldots}}$$

We may note that it is an infinite continued fraction. We may write it as

$$x = 1 + \frac{1}{x}$$

So, $x^2 = x + 1$ or $x^2 - x - 1 = 0$

It is the same quadratic equation as we obtained earlier.

So, we have $x = \frac{\sqrt{5}+1}{2}$ [ignoring the negative root]

Thus, it can be said that the golden ratio is equal to the infinite continued fraction $1+\cfrac{1}{1+\cfrac{1}{1+..}}$ in the limiting form.

3. **Golden Ratio, Continued Fraction and Sequence**

Having seen the relationship between golden ratio and the continued fraction,

$$1+\cfrac{1}{1+\cfrac{1}{1+\cfrac{1}{1+\ldots}}}$$

Let us examine the value of this fraction at different stages as shown below

Considering 1, we get the value as 1. Considering $1+\frac{1}{1}$, we get the value as $\frac{2}{1}$.

Considering $1+\cfrac{1}{1+\cfrac{1}{1}}$, we get the value as $\frac{3}{2}$.

Considering $1+\cfrac{1}{1+\cfrac{1}{1+\cfrac{1}{1}}}$, we get the value as $\frac{5}{3}$.

Considering $1+\cfrac{1}{1+\cfrac{1}{1+\cfrac{1}{1+\cfrac{1}{1}}}}$, we get the value as $\frac{8}{5}$ and so on.

Thus, the values obtained at different stages are 1, $\frac{2}{1}, \frac{3}{2}, \frac{5}{3}, \frac{8}{5}, \frac{13}{8}, \ldots$

The numerators of these values are 1, 2, 3, 5, 8, 13,...

These values depict the following pattern:

$$3 = 1 + 2,\ 5 = 2 + 3,\ 13 = 5 + 8 \text{ and so on.}$$

Note that by including 1 in the beginning, it will take the following form: 1, 1, 2, 3, 5, 8, 13,...

This is a famous sequence called the **Fibonacci sequence**.

It can be found that nth term of the Fibonacci sequence is $\frac{1}{\sqrt{5}}\left[\left(\frac{\sqrt{5}+1}{2}\right)^n - \left(\frac{-\sqrt{5}+1}{2}\right)^n\right]$

It can also be seen that in the above expression, $\left(\frac{\sqrt{5}+1}{2}\right)$ is the golden ratio.

4. **Golden Ratio and Trigonometric Ratios** It can be found that

$$\cos 36° = \sin 54° = \frac{\sqrt{5}+1}{4}$$

i.e. $$2\cos 36° = 2\sin 54° = 2\left(\frac{\sqrt{5}+1}{4}\right) = \left(\frac{\sqrt{5}+1}{2}\right) = \text{Golden ratio}$$

Thus, it can be said that twice the value of cos 36° (or twice the value of sin 54°) is equal to the golden ratio.

5. **Golden Ratio and Regular Pentagon** We know that a pentagon having all its sides and all its angles equal is called a regular pentagon. Clearly, each interior angle of a regular pentagon will be $\frac{540°}{5} = 108°$. Let us now draw any regular pentagon $ABCDE$ and draw all its diagonals AC, AD, BD, BE and CE as shown in the following figure

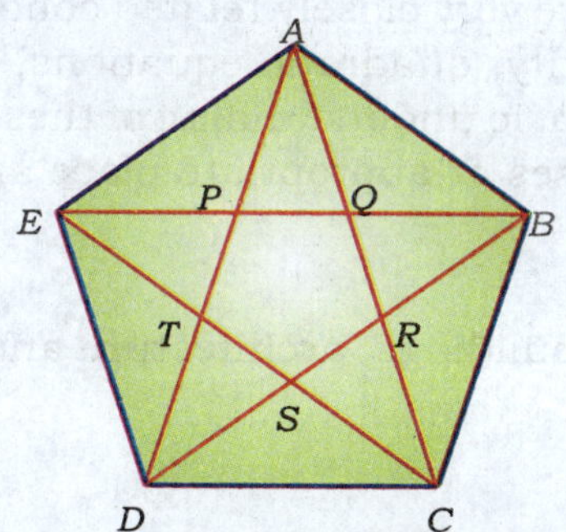

It can be observed that inside this regular pentagon, another pentagon $PQRST$ is formed. Further, this pentagon is also a regular pentagon.

It can also be seen that $\frac{AP}{PQ}, \frac{AP}{PT}, \frac{AQ}{PQ}, \frac{DS}{SR}, \ldots$ are all equal to $\frac{\sqrt{5}+1}{2}$.

i.e. the ratio of the length of the part of any diagonal not forming the side of the new pentagon on one side and the length of a side of the new pentagon is equal to the golden ratio. Further, it can also be seen that

$$\frac{AE}{AP}, \frac{AB}{BQ}, \frac{CD}{DS}, \frac{BC}{CS}, \ldots \text{ are all equal to } \frac{\sqrt{5}+1}{2}.$$

i.e. the ratio of the length of any side of the given regular pentagon and that of the part of the diagonal not forming the side of the new pentagon on one side is equal to the golden ratio.

Combining the above two results, it can be seen that in the above two regular pentagons *ABCDE* and *PQRST*,

$$\frac{AB}{PQ} = \frac{BC}{QR} = \ldots = \left(\frac{\sqrt{5}+1}{2}\right)^2 \text{ i.e. (Golden ratio)}^2$$

i.e. ratio of the corresponding sides of the two regular pentagons *ABCDE* and *PQRST* is equal to (golden ratio)^2. We also know that the ratio of the areas of two similar triangles is equal to the square of the ratio of their corresponding sides. Infact, it is true for all the similar polygons.

Further, all regular polygons are always similar.

So, it can also be said that ratio of the areas of above pentagons

$$ABCDE \text{ and} PQRST = \left(\frac{AB}{PQ}\right)^2 = \left(\frac{BC}{QR}\right)^2 = \ldots$$

$$\text{Therefore, ratio of the areas of the above two pentagons} = \left(\frac{AB}{PQ}\right)^2 = \left[\left(\frac{\sqrt{5}+1}{2}\right)^2\right]^2$$

$$= \left(\frac{\sqrt{5}+1}{2}\right)^4 = \text{(Golden ratio)}^4$$

Thus, areas of the above two regular pentagons is equal to (golden ratio)^4.

Note *The above results relating to trigonometric ratios and regular pentagons can be, infact, proved using simple trigonometrical knowledge of Class XI.*

Learning Outcome

Golden rectangle and golden ratio are very closely related concepts involving other mathematical concepts such as fractions, similarity, quadratic equations, regular pentagons, trigonometry, sequences, etc. After getting some basic understanding of these at the secondary stage, they may be studied in details in higher classes at appropriate place and time.

Application

This project is useful in designing buildings, architecture and structural engineering.

Experiment/Activity No.________ Date ________ Page No. ________

Teacher Signature ________________

Experiment/Activity No.________ Date ________ Page No. ________

Teacher Signature ________________

Experiment/Activity No.________ Date ________ Page No. ________

Teacher Signature________________

Experiment/Activity No.________ Date ________ Page No. ________

Teacher Signature ________________

Experiment/Activity No.________ Date ________ Page No. ________

Teacher Signature ________________

Experiment/Activity No.________ Date ________ Page No. ________

Teacher Signature ________________

Experiment/Activity No.________ Date ________ Page No. ________

Teacher Signature________________

Experiment/Activity No.________ Date ________ Page No. ________

Teacher Signature ________

Experiment/Activity No.________ Date ________ Page No. ________

Teacher Signature ________

Experiment/Activity No.________ Date ________ Page No. ________

Teacher Signature ________________

Experiment/Activity No.________ Date ________ Page No. ________

Teacher Signature________________

Experiment/Activity No.________ Date ________ Page No. ________

Teacher Signature ________________

Experiment/Activity No.________ Date ________ Page No. ________

Teacher Signature ________

Experiment/Activity No.________ Date ________ Page No. ________

Teacher Signature ________________

Experiment/Activity No.________ Date ________ Page No. ________

Teacher Signature________________

Experiment/Activity No.________ Date ________ Page No. ________

Teacher Signature ________

Experiment/Activity No.________ Date ________ Page No. ________

Teacher Signature ____________

Experiment/Activity No.________ Date ________ Page No. ________

Teacher Signature ________________

Experiment/Activity No.________ Date ________ Page No. ________

Teacher Signature ________

Experiment/Activity No.________ Date ________ Page No. ________

Teacher Signature ________________

Experiment/Activity No.________ Date ________ Page No. ________

Teacher Signature ________________

Experiment/Activity No.________ Date ________ Page No. ________

Teacher Signature________________

Experiment/Activity No.________ Date ________ Page No. ________

Teacher Signature ________________

Experiment/Activity No.________ Date ________ Page No. ________

Teacher Signature ________

Experiment/Activity No.________ Date ________ Page No. ________

Teacher Signature ________________

Experiment/Activity No.________ Date ________ Page No. ________

Teacher Signature ________________

Experiment/Activity No.________ Date ________ Page No. ________

Teacher Signature ________________

Experiment/Activity No.________ Date ________ Page No. ________

Teacher Signature ____________

Experiment/Activity No.________ Date ________ Page No. ________

Teacher Signature ________

Experiment/Activity No.________ Date ________ Page No. ________

Teacher Signature ________

Experiment/Activity No.________ Date ________ Page No. ________

Teacher Signature________________

Experiment/Activity No.________ Date ________ Page No. ________

Teacher Signature ________

Experiment/Activity No.________ Date ________ Page No. ________

Teacher Signature ________________

Experiment/Activity No.________ Date ________ Page No. ________

Teacher Signature ________________

Experiment/Activity No.________ Date ________ Page No. ________

Teacher Signature ________

Experiment/Activity No.________ Date ________ Page No. ________

Teacher Signature ____________

Experiment/Activity No.________ Date ________ Page No. ________

Teacher Signature ____________

Experiment/Activity No.________ Date ________ Page No. ________

Teacher Signature ________________

Experiment/Activity No.________ Date ________ Page No. ________

Teacher Signature ________

Experiment/Activity No.________ Date ________ Page No. ________

Teacher Signature ____________

Experiment/Activity No.________ Date ________ Page No. ________

Teacher Signature ________________

Experiment/Activity No.________ Date ________ Page No. ________

Teacher Signature ____________

Experiment/Activity No.________ Date ________ Page No. ________

Teacher Signature ________________

Experiment/Activity No. ________ Date ________ Page No. ________

Teacher Signature ________

Experiment/Activity No.________ Date ________ Page No. ________

Teacher Signature ________________

Experiment/Activity No.________ Date ________ Page No. ________

Teacher Signature ________

Experiment/Activity No.________ Date ________ Page No. ________

Teacher Signature ____________

Experiment/Activity No.________ Date ________ Page No. ________

Teacher Signature ________

Experiment/Activity No.________ Date ________ Page No. ________

Teacher Signature ________

Experiment/Activity No.________ Date ________ Page No. ________

Teacher Signature ________________

Experiment/Activity No.________ Date ________ Page No. ________

Teacher Signature ________________

Experiment/Activity No.________ Date ________ Page No. ________

Teacher Signature ________________

Experiment/Activity No.________ Date ________ Page No. ________

Teacher Signature ________________

Experiment/Activity No.________ Date ________ Page No. ________

Teacher Signature ____________

Experiment/Activity No.________ Date ________ Page No. ________

Teacher Signature ________

Experiment/Activity No.________ Date ________ Page No. ________

Teacher Signature ________

Experiment/Activity No.________ Date ________ Page No. ________

Teacher Signature ________________

Experiment/Activity No.________ Date ________ Page No. ________

Teacher Signature ________

Experiment/Activity No.________ Date ________ Page No. ________

Teacher Signature ________________

Experiment/Activity No.________ Date ________ Page No. ________

Teacher Signature ________

Experiment/Activity No.________ Date ________ Page No. ________

Teacher Signature________________

Experiment/Activity No.________ Date ________ Page No. ________

Teacher Signature ________

Experiment/Activity No.________ Date ________ Page No. ________

Teacher Signature ________________

Experiment/Activity No.________ Date ________ Page No. ________

Teacher Signature ________